FROM
COVER
TO
COVER

The occasional papers

of a Book Designer

Stefan Salter

ENGLEWOOD CLIFFS, NEW JERSEY

FROM COVER TO COVER

Prentice-Hall, Inc.

From Cover to Cover,
The Occasional Papers of a Book Designer

by Stefan Salter

Library of Congress Catalog Card Number: 76-80486

Printed in the United States of America • T
13-331827-3

Designed by Stefan Salter Associates

Prentice-Hall International, Inc., London; Prentice-Hall of
Australia, Pty. Ltd., Sydney; Prentice-Hall of Canada, Ltd.,
Toronto; Prentice-Hall of India Private Ltd., New Delhi;
Prentice-Hall of Japan, Inc., Tokyo.

Many of the articles in this book first appeared in the
pages of *Book Production & Bookbinding Magazine, Book
Production Industry* and *Publishers' Weekly,* and are reproduced here by permission of those publications.

For my children and for my friends

Foreword

Stefan Salter first entered our lives in August, 1942. He was then book designer for a New York printing concern, American Book-Stratford Press, and my husband, Kurt Wolff, and I were preparing the first publications for the recently founded publishing house, Pantheon Books. There were no offices at the time—for reasons of highly necessary thrift, the preliminary editorial and production work was done in our private apartment on Washington Square South.

Stefan first came to see us as a representative of the printer; soon he took the role of a personal adviser and friend. He had come to the United States in the late twenties, had an American wife, and was at home in the language and customs of a country still new and strange to us. We spoke the same language, German, and the same language also metaphorically. Stefan Salter and Kurt Wolff were both gentle people, with great friendliness and genuine concern for others. They shared an understanding of music, they both loved good food, and above all, books were, for them, not merchandise produced as economically as possible to be sold as rapidly as possible to make room for new merchandise, but objects of enduring quality, to be produced with the appropriate care.

There was more to the relationship between publisher and designer than a purely business contact. Stefan Salter once described it himself: "I was not executing somebody's orders; we were doing something together."

The first book Stefan Salter designed for Pantheon was, as I remember, Charles Péguy's *Basic Verities*, a bilingual edition of brief text passages, aphorisms and poetry. (Pantheon's first salesman predicted a maximum sale of seventy copies; fortunately, he was mistaken.) As I look at the volume today, the past comes rushing back; Stefan's leisurely visits, the thought and patience devoted to every page, every half title, the perfectly balanced running heads, the unity he created from such disparate material—French and English, prose and poetry. To this day, it is one of the most satisfying books for me to look at in its simplicity and clarity, the design unobtrusively serving the text and beautiful through its perfect service. That he was doing this kind of work, with no sense of self-importance, with the willingness to be an auxiliary to the writer, gives the measure of the man.

I doubt whether anyone working in publishing and book production today can imagine how menial were some of the things we did together for the sake of fine book-making. The willingness to do them, however, made it possible to produce, at reasonable cost both to publisher and buyer, those "rare" publications that are a delight to the connoisseur. Among these I particularly remember a portfolio of facsimile prints of Manet letters; letters that Manet had enlivened with aquarelles, a headpiece here, a vignette there, a fruit, a flower, a portrait sketch, frail and enchanting improvisations. Once reproduced, they had to be mounted on board, something that had to be done by very careful human hands.

Stefan and his wife offered to do the handwork, which otherwise might have been either poorly executed or prohibitively expensive for the firm's slender means. At the time the Salters lived in a Village brownstone. The material was delivered to them by pushcart—pushed, incidentally, by one of our closest collaborators, a man of vast erudition and certainly capable of better things.

The last book Stefan Salter designed for us was also the last book on which Kurt Wolff worked editorially: Bernard Berenson's diaries. The first was published in 1943, the last in 1964, the year after Kurt Wolff's death. During these twenty years, friendship and contact in and out of business remained constant. Two men deeply concerned with the right and fitting appearance of books, with the permanent as against the gimmicky, had met and meshed, and enhanced, I am sure, one for the other, the joy in their profession.

Helen Wolff

Contents

Preface

This book is a collection of brief essays written for the pages of *Book Production & Bookbinding Magazine*, *Book Production Industry* and *Publishers' Weekly*. They were written during the last 17 years as random thoughts of technical information. They dealt with topics never very far removed from book publishing and book production as this has been my career.

I am indebted to the publishers of the above-mentioned magazines for their permission to use the articles in book form. In particular, to the late Frank B. Myrick of the Penton Publishing Company and to Chandler B. Grannis of R. R. Bowker Company for the encouragement they have given me all along.

I owe thanks to Alfred Cain, "my" editor at Prentice-Hall, who, with Carol Cartaino, organized and edited the material with great selective skill. I am also very grateful for the encouragement and help I received from Helen Mather and Viola Sullivan in the preparation of Part One: About Myself.

It gave me a special pleasure to design this book myself.

Old Greenwich, Connecticut
S. S.

When the rags are picked, and the paper is made
  And the types in order set,
And the sheets are printed, pressed, folded and bound
  Your nice new book you will get.

from a children's card game,
Boston, 1846

A B

Part One: About Myself

C

My oldest possessions

are books. Some of them have belonged to me for over fifty years, and have survived favorite items of clothing, cherished old letters, important documents and other keepsakes that accumulate during a lifetime. These books bring back the past to me; each brings to mind incidents that might otherwise have been forgotten as well as people who have gone out of my life and places not seen for a long time.

There are some books missing from this treasured collection. Still, their absence can start me thinking about the distant years.

Such is the case with the very first book I remember. It was a book from Switzerland that told the story of an ordinary day in the life of a company of soldiers. I remember the illustrations very vividly. The first picture showed the soldiers sleeping peacefully on their cots. Through an open window the sun could be seen rising and coloring the sky. This was followed by the scene at reveille when the soldiers scrambled out of their cots and into their uniforms. Other illustrations showed the soldiers drilling, eating, and marching behind a band. Near the end a trumpeter blew taps, and finally the soldiers are seen sleeping again as in the first picture, only this time the sky was depicted as dark and the stars and the moon could be seen.

My mother read this book to me while we traveled by train to a summer place in the Alps. Mother and I were alone in the compartment because my two older brothers and my sister found better things to do than watching me being spoiled by Mother. I loved these trips, the books she read to me, and particularly the lunch. I would have a delicious crisp buttered roll and a hard-boiled egg—the salt coming from a little piece of paper—and cool lemonade from a thermos bottle would be poured into my own silver cup.

My mother (like other families from our part of town) brought along on these trips many pieces of luggage containing familiar household articles. She wore what she referred to as her gray "travel suit," a white blouse with a brooch and white gloves, all in danger of becoming soiled from the cinders which flew in through the open window. Of course, my hands had to be washed frequently as well as my face; my mother did this usually with a handkerchief. If it was very hot she might sprinkle a few drops of eau de Cologne—we called it *kölnisch Wasser*—on the handkerchief before wiping my forehead. I would feel wonderfully refreshed.

"Mama," as I remember her in those years, was, as always, very patient and kind, and a very comfortable person to be with. We sat close together so she could show me the pictures while she read the text to me. I have been trying to find that book for a long time but no one seems to remember it.

When I had learned to read, people began to give me books. I remember the *Arabian Nights* because it had such pretty pictures. They were printed in so many colors, including silver and gold, that I felt they must surely be the most beautiful pictures in the world. They must have been lithographs because I remember noticing the many little dots which created the tones and colors of the illustrations. By the time I was seven years old I began to read all kinds of books lying on my stomach on a horrible little pink sofa to which I was very attached. Sometimes my little dog, a dachshund named Beckmesser, shared the sofa with me. He was unpredictable in his moods and bit when you least expected it. Eventually he was given away to the owner of the vegetable store.

Christmas Eve it was snowing. I was sitting alone in the dark dining room watching the snowflakes come down in the courtyard of the apartment house. Our apartment was large because we were nine people, including the cook and two maids. The bedrooms were entered from a long corridor. I often rode my bike the length of it. In the front of the apartment there were four large rooms. The dining room where I sat that Christmas Eve, the living room where the tree would soon be, the music room with its grand piano, and my father's office where I was rarely allowed. Across the way I could see the other families' Christmas trees. I sat there alone because I was only eight years old and the younger children had to wait until the tree had been decorated and the gifts had been brought by the Christ-child. The best part of Christmas was always Christmas Eve. I could hear voices behind the closed sliding doors, a little light showed under the doors, but best of all I could smell the Christmas tree and the candles and the honey cake. At last a little bell was rung which meant that the Christ-child had come and gone. The doors were thrown open and I was allowed to come in. I always stopped for a moment to take in the whole picture and I think now that it must have been quite a bit like a Currier and Ives print. On the left stood a Christmas tree, a blue spruce covered with artificial snow, tinsel, burning red wax candles, and a lot of decorated cookies and chocolate rings. There were also gilt walnuts hanging from the branches and, on the very top, a much-admired little wax angel. The rest of the room was filled with little tables, each covered with a white damask cloth, which held the gifts for each member of the family. Our Christmas gifts were not wrapped, so one could see at a glance what the gifts were. I paid little attention to the other tables as I could tell easily which was mine. It was covered with toys, sweets, "practical things" which I discounted as gifts, and a little pile of books. I inspected all the toys, pushed the socks and shirts away politely, tasted some of the marzipan and *leb-kuchen* (gingerbread), and saved the books till last. We all had made a little show of admiring each other's gifts and thanking each other; the maids had come in, curtsied, and been given gifts by my parents, and in the end we had sung Christmas carols. I thought my father was very handsome on such occasions and my mother very lovely indeed with her friendly smile. I surveyed my brothers and my sister, who were from eight to twelve years older than I, more critically. They were always bossing me around. There was still a little time until Christmas supper would be served. I sat down on the floor under a lamp with my little pile of books around me and started to examine them.

For my ninth birthday I was given a little printing press. It was equipped with real type, real printer's ink, a small roller, and some cards and paper. I immediately set myself a calling card with my name and address. Everyone who came to our house had visiting cards which were left on a little silver tray. There were such names as Enrico Caruso and Arturo Toscanini and many others whose fame did not impress a little boy. I had no one to call on so I set out on a more ambitious venture. I decided to publish a weekly magazine for my twenty-two classmates at the Grunewald Real-Gymnasium. I knew that all magazines printed serialized novels so I decided to use *The Noble Blood,* a story of life in a military school, for this purpose. I even marked every fourth page in my book *(to be continued).* The story was about a cadet whom rigid discipline and intolerance had driven to death. It made me cry. My life at home was uncomplicated and I felt sorry for the cadet. I thought we might have been friends and perhaps I could have saved him.

When I had set two and a half lines of the story, the lower case "e's" gave out. Also I had managed to get my hands, my face and my shirt stained with plenty of printer's ink. My mother made me wash up and put on a clean shirt. The publishing project was given up and I never thought of it again.

"Garrone had a system for his library. Whenever he could afford a new book, he took it to the bookbinder and had it bound in bookcloth of a solid color. For adventure he used green, for history blue. Inspirational books were done in white and stories in red. He arranged the books according to the color so that his library was very colorful." This account comes from De Amici's *Heart,* an Italian children's book, a great favorite of mine when I was a youngster. It dealt with history, particularly that of the new Italy of Garibaldi, family, inspirational thoughts and short stories that would interest young boys. It managed to describe life in a little Italian town and, particularly, in an elementary school. I realized then what different lives boys could lead.

The four years of World War I had left my little world undisturbed. My older brothers had become soldiers and both had come home unharmed. I knew of no one who had been killed or even wounded. In a town such as Berlin there seemed to be no suffering or need beyond shortages of materials and food. We schoolchildren collected acorns for the animals in the zoo and tinfoil to be melted for bullets. In and out of school we boys read only of the glorious exploits of our armies and navies. When the war was lost and the armistice signed, the soldiers came back.

One day at school we suddenly heard military music through an open window. Soldiers were marching by. Regardless of rigid school discipline we ran out in front of the school. The teachers could not hold us back so they followed us out. Outside an unending line of regiments was marching by, bands in front, flags flying.

Some of us boys marched along. It was miles before I discovered that I was in another part of town. To let some traffic pass by the soldiers had come to temporary halt. I noticed a woman dressed in black

standing on the sidewalk and holding onto a boy
who was wearing a black armband. In her other
arm she carried a little girl. The child was laughing
and the woman was crying. I suddenly knew for
whom she was crying. I could not march any longer
and went home slowly.

When I was twelve I "reached the goal of the class,"
which meant that I was transferred to the seventh
grade. My first trip was to the school bookstore
which was located a few blocks from the school.
There I was allowed to look at the new books. The
book dealer gave us a list of the new books required
in seventh grade and what they would cost. Books
were not free nor were they bought secondhand.
Although I wasn't looking forward to hard homework and difficult lessons, the new books always
intrigued me. For one thing they were so very fresh
and it seemed to add to my prestige to use the books
of the next class up. The books I liked least were
math books.

A few years ago I found a beautiful Euclid which
was printed in four colors around 1840. Would I
not have done much better in geometry if I had
been inspired by it? The discipline to which a European schoolchild was exposed in my youth was strict
and sometimes frightening, and I believe that hard-
to-read textbooks and hard benches to sit on were
part of it. Going to the other extreme of making

seats and books too soft may not produce results either, but the years I spent with my schoolbooks have clearly been the cause of my near-obsession for trying to make textbooks especially readable and attractive.

The railroad bridge was on my way to school. I was in seventh grade and because a general strike had been called I had to walk three miles to school. One morning when I was about to cross the bridge, I noticed that some of the pavement had been dug up at the entrance to the bridge, and that a machine gun stood pointed in the direction from which I was coming. Two steel-helmeted soldiers sat behind it and when they saw how scared I was they waved me on good-naturedly. "Go on to school, kid," they yelled, "we ain't gonna harm you." It was in the days of a right-wing Putsch and there was much excitement in the school, but we had to settle down for a very dull history lesson. The only good thing about history was the brand-new history book which I loved because it had many pictures. I realized with horror that I had forgotten to bring the book to school. When the teacher called on me I had to admit it and, what was worse, I did not remember my assignment at all. The teacher was very angry. In the years to come, I learned other history lessons, many of them right in the streets.

At home we were not very much concerned with

history or, so it seems to me, with current events. Friends, relatives, and neighbors all said "We are not interested in politics." They felt this statement absolved them from any responsibility and protected them from any danger. They kept saying it until it was too late. As for us boys, we knew a great deal about sports, some of us began to know something about girls, but most of us were "not interested in politics" either.

"You need a label, too," said the bookbinder. He had helped me to select materials to bind a set of Dickens which were only bound in paper. I had saved for a long time to buy the set and have it bound. Usually it was left to the bookbinder, who was also the book dealer, to use his own judgment, but I was fourteen years old and I wanted to select the binding materials myself.

I settled on a red patterned paper for the side, black calico for the backbone and corners, brown end papers, and a little red leather label on which the titles were to be stamped in gold. I still have the set in my library. It was my first design. One of the titles, *The Christmas Carol*, is still in paper; it was not bound like the others. I don't remember whether I had forgotten to take it along or whether I ran out of money and had to wait until I had saved some. At any rate, it remains in paper still, a silent reminder of an unfinished job.

There was an aura of music and the theater about our home which I took quite for granted. We actually had two grand pianos in two separate music rooms. One was used by my father when he auditioned singers and one by my sister who practiced, it seemed interminably, the lengthy passages of Chopin and Mendelssohn. At one time her piano was used by a young Chilean boy who was studying in Berlin. His name was Claudio Arrau and if I ever had any ambition to become a musician he killed it for me. He was tirelessly practicing all morning and all afternoon. In later years I was not a bit surprised to find that he had become famous. But in those days I wished he wouldn't always play the same piece.

Perhaps he also discouraged my sister, for somehow the second grand disappeared and in its stead my brother George set up a miniature theater. It was a great deal more elaborate than a toy theater and quite a bit larger. He had designed and constructed it himself. As my brother had always been interested in stage design, this was a great way to work at his hobby, and I know that eventually it helped him to get his first job as assistant set designer for the State Opera Company. During the years of this and subsequent jobs as stage designer, he made fascinating miniature sets of scenery. Everything was working on the stage even including an iron curtain and an intricate system of stage lighting. He gave up his career as a stage designer in favor of becoming a book jacket designer. In the meantime, my sister was working in a bookstore and my other brother had become a partner in a publishing house. I had many opportunities to go to the theater, but one early experience stands out in my memory.

My father had at that time turned to arranging entire "seasons" of Italian opera, Russian theater, and the Warsaw Ballet. The companies traveled all over Europe, particularly from one theater to another in the many German towns. The companies usually started from Berlin and one day my father took me to a performance of the Warsaw Ballet. As my father had some business with the stage manager, he simply took me on stage and left me there in the wings for the duration of the performance. I was standing, naturally, out of the vision of the audience but I could see what was happening on the stage.

The sets were in place when I came and by and by the lights went on. One could hear the murmur of the audience and the tuning of the orchestra in front of the curtain.

As I watched, fascinated, a number of dancers came from the back of the stage and arranged themselves in poses right in front of my eyes. I had never seen such beautiful creatures. Men and women alike were made up in a way I had never seen before. I didn't realize at that moment that their red lips and cheeks and that their eyebrows had to be visible from as far away as the second balcony.

The women I had known were relatives, or friends of my parents, or young girls I had seen in the homes of school friends. Few of them had been attractive and, of course, none wore any costumes or even a little make-up. At least, I didn't notice it if they did.

I had seen acrobats before, and some of the kids at school were pretty good gymnasts, but the motion I saw before my eyes after the curtain rose was so full of grace and imagination that I was over-whelmed. When the curtain fell and rose again to the applause of the audience I wanted to applaud too, but I was too embarrassed. The curtain came down for the last time and the dancers slowly left the stage, arm in arm, talking rapidly in Polish, a language I did not understand. Some smiled at me and I answered by bowing a little as every German school-boy does when he is greeted by an older person.

When I was fifteen or sixteen years old my family spent the summer in Switzerland. My father had to go on to Milan to meet Arturo Toscanini and he took me along on this trip. My father was an im-presario who represented the Metropolitan Opera Company of New York in Europe. In his youth he had been First Cellist under Gustav Mahler in Ham-burg. My father was a kind man and he took a par-ticular interest in me since I was the youngest and still open to suggestion. Besides, I was the only one who cared about his business at all. Milan in the

summer heat, and talk about singers, did not hold
my interest for very long and my father, noticing
this, sent me on my own to Venice. Perhaps this was
to test my independence. In my city clothes, I sat
squeezed between sausage-eating and wine-drinking
paisanos in a third-class compartment. I was embarrassed, uncomfortable, and very hungry and
thirsty and there was no food to be had on the train.
But when I arrived in Venice I was enchanted. What
a fascinating town it was for a German boy; a town
of old buildings, of waterways and gondolas, with
no automobiles in the streets. I knew very little
Italian and I assumed that the Venetian way of
speaking was medieval. I simply thought that life in
this town had not changed. The food was all new to
me, the moon over St. Mark was enormous and
blood-red, and I had never been alone before in a
foreign country. There was mosquito netting over
my bed in the hotel room and the strange noises at
night scared me. I was glad when my father arrived
a day or two later.

All this came back to me when I was designing a
book called *This Was Toscanini*. I believe this book
is among my best and I think that some of the hot
days in Milan, the trip in the third-class carriage to
Venice, and the wandering through the narrow
passageways of Venice shows in this book. Perhaps
you don't see it, but I do.

I went to a boys' school for twelve years. The nearest girls' school was half a mile away. All the same, some of the girls would occasionally walk past our school, presumably on their way home. In the winter we threw snowballs at them; in the spring, nice prickly chestnuts, and in the fall just pebbles. The chestnuts were aimed at their bare legs since they wore socks like the boys. The snowballs were meant to hit their pigtails or even their noses, and the pebbles were intended for the rest of their anatomy. If we missed them they laughed, made faces or even stuck their tongues out. If we hit, they let out howls and threats, but they continued to walk the detour which took them three or four blocks out of their way. It took me more time than I care to admit to figure out this puzzle. No matter what efforts were made by either side it did not produce the desired result of a friendly meeting, leading hopefully to a friendship between the boys and girls.

When I was ready for such a friendship I conferred with my best friend. We both admitted to each other that we saw no way of getting to know girls. An idea came to me. I remembered a girl to whom I was introduced when I was eleven and she barely ten. As we were not even neighbors, we couldn't or wouldn't be bothered to make friends. I now proceeded to find her telephone number and called her.

"Miss Margot," I stammered, "my mother has

asked me to call you and inquire if you would like to take dance lessons which she is going to arrange." This was not true, of course, and, incidentally, it was never discussed thereafter, but she said sweetly, "Thank you so very much, but I couldn't possibly. I am being confirmed this year you know," she added importantly. After talking for a while she told me that her mother had suggested that I pay a visit to them the next Sunday afternoon. I did, with a bunch of pink carnations and in great embarrassment.

But we did become friends and after a while we began to go to the theater or to concerts together. Margot had sweet blue eyes and a pair of dimples. She was a very pretty girl with a great sense of humor. I longed to be with her but whenever we met, I became shy and we rarely even held hands. Sometimes I had tickets to the opera where my brother was employed as a scenic designer. My father had so many connections with the world of music and the theater that all these tickets were complimentary. All I needed was subway fare and a little extra for incidentals. Our subway was clean and colorful. Second-class cars were red and the seats upholstered in red leather. The third-class cars were yellow with wooden benches. The doors had to be closed by the conductor before the trains could leave. There were no express trains. After the theater, we took the "underground," as the subway was called, to a certain station. She stayed on the train to the end of the line and I had to change to another train. It would have been nice to take her all the way home but it would have been too late for me to get home by train and I had no money for a taxi.

My allowance in those days was not big enough to buy whatever I liked nor did I have any ways of earning money, so that I had to plan expenditures to match my allowance. One day I browsed in a bookstore hoping to find a little book as a birthday gift for my girl. I saw a slender volume bound in parchment and of a peculiar bright blue color which reminded me instantly of her eyes. The title of the book was stamped in silver and the entire book was printed in italics in a beautiful shade of blue. I had never seen that before but it appealed to me. It was a Persian love story and set me back three weeks' allowance.

I often browsed in bookstores and one day I came across a small book titled *The Idea*. At seventeen I, too, was full of ideas. They were on education, comforts, and science. Some were standard, some unusual, and most were unworkable. So I picked up the book and was quite surprised to find that it consisted entirely of woodcuts without any text whatsoever. It was the work of the Flemish wood engraver Frans Masareel and very powerful in its composition, content, and massive texture. This is one of the books which has never lost its appeal for me. It tells the story of a man whose creative mind sends an idea out in the world hoping for its acceptance, but finds it rejected, maligned, and misunderstood. Eventually the idea, depicted as a woman, returns to him to escape a hostile world, only to find him hopefully and fondly gazing at another idea he has created.

It was the jacket of a book displayed in the window of a bookstore which attracted my attention. It was a photomontage and I had never seen anything like it before. When I opened the book and read a page or two I became fascinated. It was Upton Sinclair's *The Jungle*. I took it home and began to read it sitting at my table.

My mother came into the room and asked me to let her use the table to cut a pattern. I placed the book on the windowsill, then I remained standing in front of it and continued to read. When my mother had finished I did not go back to the table but read until it became too dark. It was the first time I had read a class-conscious book. It made me think.

Whenever we went away for the summer or whenever we took my father to the station as he was going away on business, I looked forward to the book-vending machine. It sold inexpensive paper-covered books. The list of published titles was enormous although the vending machine was limited to sixteen different books. The prices varied with the length of the book and the titles took in just about anything I could imagine. It was my fondest dream to own all of those books. They were designed conventionally. When I design paperbacks today I often think of the vending machine and I try to make the paperback look as interesting as possible.

All through my childhood, I had traveled with my family to the Alps. We usually stayed in a large, comfortable hotel which, however, was almost unbearably dull for a youngster, especially on rainy days. We stayed in these summer-vacation spots usually for a solid six weeks. The routine was always the same: breakfast, lunch, and dinner in the big dining hall at the same table, with rather predictable food. In between, a walk in the morning, a visit to the village, perhaps the pastry shop in the afternoon. There were hours during the day when I was not to disturb my parents. Both rested after lunch, which was the big meal of the day, and part of the day my father was busy reading newspapers or writing business letters. My mother was more accessible, but it just wasn't enough. There were, of course, many other children in such hotels, but if you weren't in a group you were out of luck.

I remember one summer in particular because there was at least some excitement during a particular rainy weekend. All the parents had disappeared into their rooms after lunch and all the children had assembled in the dining hall which also served as a ballroom and was used for concerts and other festive occasions. At one end of the room there was, surprisingly enough, a gambling machine, the kind known as a "one-armed bandit." I remember the plums, cherries, and lemons quite distinctly to this day. You threw a Swiss franc into the machine, for this happened in St. Moritz, turned the crank and the machine rewarded you occasionally with a meager return of one, two, or three francs.

This day a small group of older boys was standing around the machine. They had pooled their resources and, after they had cranked three or four times and lost all, one of them had pushed the machine in disgust and the machine had reacted in the most magnificent manner. It changed its position to the jackpot and a great many francs rolled crashing into the pocket. The boys were overjoyed. They immediately invested another franc, turned the handle and jackpot it was again. And again and again luck favored them. By this time all of us from the fourteen-year-old down to the toddlers pressed close to the machine and clamored for a turn.

How can I describe what the rain of silver meant to the children? It would buy untold quantities of goodies in the shops, things that children dream of but can never buy for themselves.

The older boys reluctantly turned over the machine to the rest of us, but the excitement somehow attracted the *portier*. He was a big, imposing man in a magnificent uniform. He was, in effect, a combination doorman, desk clerk, and manager. When he realized what was happening he hung a sign on the machine which said "Out of Order," shooed the protesting mob out of the ballroom, and locked the doors.

Things like that didn't happen every summer and neither the grandeur of the mountains which, however, included tedious dusty walks, nor the fine cuisine attracted me much more after I was fourteen or fifteen.

I had heard of "Holiday Fellowships" where you could spend the summers with groups of young people, male and female, away from parents and tedium. After I had obtained a folder or two—they were always printed in green ink—I made a reservation for myself and my friend, Max Fromm. Our parents were pleased with our initiative and probably just as happy to get away from us.

Max and I spent two lovely summers in these camps in England and France. They were run by some English church-people in great austerity but also with warm and sincere cheerfulness. As Germans, only a few years after the war had ended, we were uneasy, but we were received kindly and made many friends. These trips acquainted us with a number of regions, both in France and England, and of course, with Paris and London.

The time had come to leave home. I was nineteen. I had graduated from a good school with some distinction and I wanted to explore the world and myself.

It was natural that I left my home to go to England, which I had become fond of, and settled in London, finding myself a room as a "paying guest."

There was no pressing need to do anything specific immediately, but when, after a few weeks of becoming acquainted with London, I found myself in front of the County Council School of Arts and Crafts, I walked in and registered as a student. This visit had not been planned and yet I don't think it was entirely by chance. At home the accent of living had always been on music, literature, and art. Now, as I stood in front of the attractive and simple posters which outlined what the student might learn in this school, I knew that I wanted to study here. This is where I had my first lessons in typography, learned the basic principles of printing, and studied bookbinding with the famous English bookbinder Douglas Cockerell. The equipment of the school was deliberately limited. Only one type face was available, however, in many sizes and each classroom had many full cases of it. The type face was, of course, Caslon. We also had only two types of presses, the conventional small job presses and the small flat bed book presses. The equipment used to learn the art of bookbinding was relatively simple.

It included a sewing frame, clamps and vises, folding bones, glue pots and hammers for rounding, and a small selection of stamping tools such as the semi-circular filets, individual ornamental brass dies, and line-producing rollers. There was enough brass type for stamping but it was not particularly attractive. What was attractive, though, were the wonderful marble papers which Douglas Cockerell turned out and which he taught us to fabricate, too. I doubt that there is a binder left in this day and age who will make his own marble papers. This was the first time I realized what infinite care had to be taken in paring the thick leather down to a thinness which could be bent around a heavy board. The boards, too, had to be cut individually and accurately. Naturally, the stamping had to be right or else the whole binding was spoiled.

The school itself was an unattractive building. I remember the students' room where we spent our lunch periods eating a sandwich or a pork-pie. In the center of the room there was a Ping-Pong table. The rule which allowed the winner of the first game to stay until he was beaten by one of the challengers was in my favor. I was a champ at Ping-Pong.

I have seen many picture books in my life, beautiful ones, interesting ones, and even amusing ones. But never before or since, such an impressive one as *Deutschland, Deutschland über Alles.* This was the book which made it abundantly clear to me, a young man who knew nothing about politics or economics, that there was trouble brewing. Naturally, I did not know exactly what was about to happen, but the author of the book, Kurt Tucholsky, and the illustrator, John Hartfield, knew. A few years later they just barely escaped with their lives. What impressed me at once about the book were the photographs, the photomontages and the way the text ran with the illustrations. Dramatic statements were made not only by text or illustrations but by the way they were laid out. It was a great textbook of our time, teaching important lessons which few people were willing to learn. It was like the handwriting on the wall and it sent me away forever and in ample time.

My first years in America were the years of the Depression. During the winter of 1931 I could not find any job. In the summer of 1932 I became a cook in a children's camp. It was a good summer for me but as I had not been paid any money at all I faced the next winter with uncertainty. I managed to get by doing some work for a printer. After awhile he and I built a little, very primitive press to print small posters using linoleum cuts which I prepared. They were printed for political clubs and small stores and I enjoyed working on them since I had a pretty free hand in designing them. I remember using textured doormats as well as linoleum which I heated in the stove to soften. The stove served also as my only source of heat because I lived in a cold-water flat. When the winter came, neither sleeping nor working was very comfortable. I spent all my available time at the library. It was cosy and bright there and I learned much of America by reading Dreiser, Sinclair Lewis, and Upton Sinclair. I also read Willa Cather and Edith Wharton. In those days I spent little time looking for attractive books, for fine typography, or beautiful bindings. I read incessantly and I knew only a few type faces by name.

As soon as I could manage it I left New York to go to California. I meant to escape the winter and poverty. Life in California was made a great deal more bearable by the fine weather and by the fact that you need less clothing and spent much less on food. I soon found a job in a bake shop icing pastries at night and tried to sleep by day, next door to an elementary school. Eventually, I was able to find a job reading foreign books—in German, French, and Italian—for the story departments of Paramount Pictures and Warner Brothers. It paid very little but enough to live quite comfortably. I made many friends in and out of the studios and I became interested in fine printing again. Eventually I was employed by a printer but the times were still so bad that we never knew if and when we would be paid. But even those years went by and finally I returned to New York and began my career as a book designer.

It was high time, for I was thirty years old and I was tired of working hard at uninteresting jobs for very little pay.

When I was a boy I had read glowing accounts of the men who had started as laborers and became bridge builders and of the newsboys who became newspaper magnates. I knew that things would not work quite like that, but what I didn't know was how careers are made and sustained and how they end.

No matter what these years had meant to me and everybody else they had added another side to my personality. They had taught me to be hopeful and to be resourceful.

In the fall of 1937 I was offered a job in New York to assist a book designer and so I came back. The Depression was not entirely over, but things were brightening.

Happily, free transportation was provided in the shape of a Packard limousine which we—a friend of mine from the print shop and I—were to drive from Pasadena to New York. We were even given cash for gasoline and my friend's sister supplied us with sandwiches and hard-boiled eggs for the first lap of the trip. We drove the first one thousand miles to Albuquerque in one sitting, stopping only occasionally for a brief rest. As we had to cross the Mojave Desert, we had taken a cake of ice along which came out of a vending machine at the gas station in California, but by the time we were in the desert we realized how cold it was at night. Our homemade air-conditioning turned to our disadvantage. It froze to the floorboard and could not be dislodged.

When I arrived in New York I found out that the job was not waiting for me, but I was waiting for the job. However, a few weeks later I did begin my career as book designer.

Everything was beautifully new to me. Sharing a private office instead of sitting in a corner, having at my disposal hundreds of type faces, where before I had to satisfy myself with the contents of a few rickety cases of hand type, was pleasure enough. I also enjoyed working in an office with forty or fifty other people all presumably as interested in books as I was. But that was not all. Part of the floor and another floor were filled with thundering presses and wondrous bindery equipment. There were batteries of women sewing unending streams of books together. There were staples of bookcloth in all colors and powerful presses stamping book titles on the covers.

In the basement there were carloads upon carloads of beautiful white paper. On another floor the finished books lay in bins or were packed on skids ready for their voyages to the bookshop and to the readers. There is something fascinating in seeing so many copies of the same title. It is almost like being present at the birth of a new idea or a great invention. It was an absolute paradise for me. To this day, every time I pick up a new book I have the same feeling of being on the threshold of a new experience.

I don't recall ever wanting to be a fireman or an ice cream vendor, but I know that in the years when I first thought of a career I was considering three of them simultaneously. The first was that of a stage director, the second of a graphic designer, and the last, very simply, to be a publisher. In the end I believe I was able to combine them.

The first great lesson that I had to learn was that of humility. Working in small print shops and making do with poor equipment had not spoiled me, but all that time I had secretly yearned for the day when I could use the paper and the type and the production methods which I really admired. I had to see now that while all were quite available there were many obstacles that could come between them and me. The three most obvious ones were elements of cost, time, and of the customer's taste. The cost, naturally, was the paramount thing in those days. But as cost began to assume less importance, the time element became more important. The customer's taste is an intangible, of course, and it has largely been a question of who he trusted more in such matters—me or himself. It became necessary for me to revise my opinions. Perhaps what I had been believing in regard to typography was not necessarily the best way. Perhaps I would have to change my ideas on bookcloth and other materials and, perhaps, even on book design.

In the spring of 1938 I was given my first solid assignment, that of designing three companion volumes, *Skyways, Through by Rail,* and *The Mail Comes Through.*

I was given a free hand with these books and they stand out clearly in my memory as having been a challenge which I met, a challenge to artistic and technical know-how, and most of all to resourcefulness.

All three books consisted of relatively short manuscripts typed on yellow paper. All were to be illustrated in some fashion which was left to me, and to be made into "supplementary readers" for use in elementary schools.

It was the very thing I loved to do and still do because it involved my interests in transportation, history, and even philately. The credit lines under the many illustrations are witnesses to the many places and organizations I had to contact to obtain them. For *Skyways* I went to Newark Airfield and had a pilot explain the instrument board as well as I could comprehend it, as well as give me a very elementary lesson in landing patterns. I had to go to Washington, D.C., where I had much help from the Smithsonian Institution, the General Post Office, and from the Association of American Railroads. But I also discovered a wonderful collection of early railroad posters at Columbia University, and I made a number of decorative two-color borders out of a variety of my own postage stamps. Naturally, many photographs came from the usual commercial sources and, of course, the Bettmann Archives.

When I look at these books these days I feel that, unlike many of my products that date back that far, these are practically flawless. Of course, I can detect certain faults but, then again, they were overcome by so much freshness and enthusiasm that it would be very hard for me to duplicate them now that I am not a naïve beginner anymore.

Skyways was selected for the "Fifty Books of the Year," for the Textbook Show, and also in a more informal selection which was made by some designers every month.

A year later I joined this group of designers. We met once a month at the offices of *Publishers' Weekly* where we looked over hundreds of books published in the previous month which were kept on shelves waiting to be catalogued.

We had to work fast as there were many books to be looked at. However, in those days so little attention was given to good design that the four of us could weed out the majority of the titles. We were probably left with forty to fifty books from which we separated about a dozen, and after some consideration and a bit of horse-trading, settled on four or five. These books were not necessarily beautiful, but there was something to recommend them for design or materials or production methods, or perhaps a combination of all of these. One of us would take the chosen ones home and write an article about them. This was also a way of building up our libraries as we often made only feeble efforts to return them. Our judgments, I believe, were fair and, as it is proper for judges and teachers, we often encouraged less experienced publishers. "Not bad for XYZ Publishers," we would say, and make an effort in our article to point out what could have been better.

There were publishers then, as now, who appreciated good design and who encouraged everything that could be done for it, but there were also some who seemed to be absolutely disinterested. Two of the three largest publishers in New York seemed to think of "design" as a dirty word then. Today their books are among the very best designed.

Two years after I had established myself as a book designer I became a husband and, a few years later, a father. As my life became more rounded, my time and affection could no longer be devoted entirely to books. But I believe that the books did not lose out for, from here on, I could talk about my work at home and eventually my children served me to understand their growing taste and interest for books from their point of view.

There was time for travel and time for cultural interests but also for sports and for friendships. Our interests expressed themselves in hunting antiques, learning to play the recorder, and even going back to stamp collecting, a love dormant for the many years since my childhood. Those were the carefree days when my job was still a nine-to-five proposition; when my wife and I had all the time we wanted to ourselves, such as going to the World's Fair, which from our home in Kew Gardens was practically around the corner, or going for long walks on Saturdays or Sundays. It never occurred to us to have a car or perhaps we couldn't afford it. My salary was forty dollars a week. I don't remember how much rent we paid, but I do remember a three or four months' "concession"; that is, not having to pay rent for that amount of time. I remember shopping for the weekend and spending about four to five dollars which included big roasts, or going to the farm stand just one block from us where a dozen ears of corn—and the man always gave us thirteen —cost ten cents, and I remember that I produced a "defense workers' dinner" for less than one dollar. At that time, my wife worked at a turret lathe (it was before our children were born), making more money than I did. I very gladly cooked dinner since she came home an hour later than I. I prided myself for an artistic flair for thinking up unusual menus and cooking them rather rapidly. I am not sure now whether the limit of one dollar, self-imposed as it was, was for the entire dinner or per head, especially since I often served some wine with it. But it was a lot of fun for me and we joked a lot about it.

On Sundays we lounged in typical New York fashion all day reading *The New York Times* and sometimes going to a movie in the evening. In the afternoon we always listened to the New York Philharmonic.

It was such a Sunday, on December seventh, that the broadcast was interrupted and the news of Pearl Harbor was flashed over the air. It took a long while for us to understand it.

Just as we had been stunned by the sudden Nazi invasion of Northern Europe, we were quite unprepared again for the present disaster. I believe it was that very same night, or perhaps a day or two later, that we were awakened by the unfamiliar sound of hundreds of sirens over Queens. We could see innumerable searchlights stabbing the night sky. After a while, the all-clear came through and the "unidentified aircraft" was never identified.

Two nights before Pearl Harbor we had had two couples for dinner. They were neighbors and we were beginning to become good friends with them. One of the men was a musician playing the xylophone over WNYC, New York's broadcasting station, and the other one was a manager in an import and export firm. Their wives were sisters, daughters of a respected doctor. The men were Japanese, the women were born in the United States of Japanese parents and could not even speak Japanese. All four and their children were rounded up the day after Pearl Harbor and in turn, after some weeks, they were exchanged for Americans coming from Japan. I still have a very kind letter from one of the women telling us that they chose to accompany their husbands to Japan where, in the end, they were treated rather as enemies because they could not speak Japanese, and where, toward the end of the war, three of their group died in the bombings. I remember what a very lovely evening we spent and that we had learned much from them that was interesting and very foreign.

The war was felt even in the publishing industry; people were drafted, materials became scarce, and books on the war were produced very rapidly. Of course we were involved now in a global war and I felt that I could well serve the country by becoming an interpreter. I made three attempts to enlist in this capacity which would also have given me the rank of first lieutenant or perhaps captain. The Army Specialist Corps, which had been functioning as a semi-civilian adjunct to the Armed Forces, was dissolved in the spring of 1942 and absorbed by the Army. I tried my luck with the Army but did not impress them with my knowledge of French and perhaps they suspected me of being a spy. As far as the Navy was concerned, they would take no one who had not been a citizen for at least ten years. As I had been a citizen for only a few years, I had very little choice but to wait. Eventually I was drafted in the same year, reported for my physical, was rejected, and sent home with a 4F.

The war-years came and passed for us as they had for me when I was a boy. I have often thought that I would have preferred to live in more peaceful times, times which might have been dedicated to study and travel. Actually, I have traveled a good deal in my time, although only on this continent and in Europe. There were, however, two occasions when I wanted to go to the Far East.

The first time was during the Depression. At the time, I lived in Los Angeles and inquired about immigrating to Japan. The very polite official of the Nipon Yusen Kaisha, Japan's shipping line, smilingly informed me that I could not obtain a third-class ticket on a Japanese boat. As he put it, I would be unable to live and eat Japanese-style. The cost of a first-class ticket was quite beyond my reach. This was shortly before the "Axis" and I think that, for a former German National, arriving in Japan might have seemed much like a trip to a concentration camp.

The second time was shortly before Pearl Harbor. I had been in contact with the Dutch government hoping to be appointed as a designer for the Dutch-Javanese government printing office in Batavia. Had I succeeded in obtaining this position, I might have found myself among the Japanese after all, but under the most unfavorable circumstances.

In my career as a book designer I have been on the staffs of only two firms, American Book-Stratford Press and H. Wolff Manufacturing Co. In 1942 I left American Book to join H. Wolff—as these two houses are usually referred to—only because working for the latter would bring me into contact with other publishers and somewhat different printing methods. Altogether, I spent ten years as an art director for two of the best book manufacturers, acquiring a good part of my technical knowledge and forming many friendships in the industry.

In these years I was designing many kinds of books, but one, designed only a few weeks after my son was born, is very fresh in my memory.

I refer to a book published as a memorial to President Franklin D. Roosevelt just three days after his death. For all the haste, the project had dignity; all persons connected with the book offered their services free, and the publisher was using up a considerable part of his war-time paper quota without deriving any profit from it. The Warm Springs Foundation was intended to be the beneficiary of this effort, but, surprisingly, the offer was turned down, needlessly and, I thought, brusquely. (More of the production details for this book are given in a later chapter.)

The war was over—the second World War in my lifetime. If I added the revolution in Berlin, the terrible inflation, and the equally horrible experience of The Great Depression, to say nothing of the rise and fall of Mussolini and Hitler and the horrors of the Spanish Civil War, I felt that the last thirty years had meant a great deal of bad news to me.

It is quite impossible to realize immediately how involved you are with what is happening around you when it happens. You survive it somehow, that is if you do, and simultaneously you gain and lose a little. I was looking forward to a more peaceful existence, a life of accomplishment and a wish to bring up a family in a home of my own.

Ten years at American and at H. Wolff had done a great deal for me. They had given me experience and self-confidence, but the time came to break away from the security and limitation of being employed. I became a free lance.

By local terms I approached the state of being a "genius" which is applied by residents of suburban communities, such as Old Greenwich, to people who earn a substantial part of their income working at home. The "commuters" are a resigned lot making the 7:58 in the morning and coming back on the 5:16. And the "clam-diggers" are the local people who never go to the city, except to the Ice Follies, and who make their living on the other two groups. They and their families have stayed put for generations and are the only true natives. The other two are always on the move, coming and going.

After a while being a free lance becomes a sort of a job. You assume new responsibilities and get involved with your house and the Boy Scouts. But it becomes a fuller life, too. In the following years I enjoyed travel, study, accomplishment, success, and failure.

Quite early in my free-lance career, I was commissioned to design and lay out a seven-thousand page encyclopedia. This was an ambitious project, technically not too difficult, but it tried my patience very severely. However, the proceeds of this job made a move to the country feasible. Some time later I was given an even bigger encyclopedia to do which enabled me to take my family to Europe for half a year.

I had not been in Europe in twenty years, but I had been longing to see it again. Some of what I saw I liked but I was convinced that I would not return to live there, as it would have meant the disruption of my career.

Quite naturally, many of my happiest experiences during that visit were meetings with publishers, visits to book stores and museums, and seeing old friends. I had lost many, but some were still there.

With the exception of Switzerland and, in particular, the French-speaking towns of Geneva and Lausanne, books manufactured in other countries were still made with poor materials. But the Swiss books were magnificent. They had not been touched by the war at all.

I made the selection of Swiss books and showed them under the auspices of the American Institute of Graphic Arts as a travel show. Through the last years I had become active in the A.I.G.A. and some years later became a director of the Institute for a few years.

I have always felt that the Institute and similar organizations have done a great deal to make people appreciate books and graphic arts and it has surprised me that such organizations get only minimal support from the industry for whom they are doing so much.

It isn't possible for me to describe the books of those years that I felt particularly attached to, because there have been so many of them. It would seem a little bit like the venerable Mr. Chips reciting a long list of graduates on his death bed. When I was still interested in records and statistics of this order, I figured that I had designed books for over a hundred publishers and it is possible that in thirty-odd years I have designed between 1500 and 2000 books. They have been very different in scope and the publishers varied in taste and demands, but I am close to all of them.

In the early sixties I realized that my eyesight was failing. Discouragement set in when it became apparent to me that I could not tell type faces and sizes from one another. I withdrew from my work and, in the end, refused to accept any more orders. I became stagnant for a year or two. I tried to comfort myself by writing my column called "Designer's Corner" and working on other writing projects.

Eventually I had enough of this inactive life and decided that I could go on designing practically as always. And with the help of a talented assistant I have been doing just that, "dictating" my designs and rebuilding a career which has meant so much to me. It has been a great exercise in patience, memory, and concentration, but it has been worth it.

Perhaps I should elaborate on this period. It may seem that the activity of designing requires vision but I found that design is the organization of graphic thoughts. Such organization can be undertaken without actually seeing a manuscript or a layout. For years I have had to be able to correct or improve designs over the telephone, for instance. A skillful designer stores away so many facts in his mind that he does not need to refer to type, paper or cloth samples because he can visualize different type faces and type sizes as well as textures of paper and colors or textures of book cloth.

When I realized the necessity of continuing my work without actually seeing it, it became apparent to me that all I needed were the eyes of an intelligent person who could analyze for me a manuscript, read the directives from the publisher, and in turn, take my dictation for the specifications I could work out in my mind. Added to that, of course, was the responsibility of producing rough or comprehensive layouts, doing some lettering, and occasionally cropping and preparing illustrations following my instructions.

It certainly was an unexpected challenge but a rewarding one. Since it became necessary to teach my assistant practically everything that I had learned myself in the last 30 years, it was certainly not easy either on me nor on a most willing but sometimes understandably confused student. It required tremendous concentration on both our parts and a great deal of patience with each other. It was often frustrating not being able to help or to do the job myself, but it was also immensely gratifying to hold the finished book in my hands and to understand that it reflected a beloved skill which I had not lost.

DE

Part Two: Life as a Free Lance

FG

Twenty years ago

my boy said: "My pop *be*signs books in a plane!"
I still do, although mostly in my studio, and preferably on a large desk. I don't really *be*sign them as he
said then, but to be quite accurate, I *design* them. In
the years that have passed much has happened even
in the little world of books. It was also twenty years
ago that promises were made to perfect a typesetting
machine smaller than a desk that could be operated
by any intelligent typist. Twenty years ago many
technological promises were made—and not kept.
Twenty years ago, prices of materials and costs of
production had gone so far that they couldn't possibly go farther—they did. And twenty years ago I
decided to become a free-lance designer.

On the face of it things looked foolproof. My office hours were my own. I could work when and as
I wanted. If I felt I deserved a raise I would talk to
myself and magnanimously grant me a modest one.
I foresaw few catches. This does not mean, however,
that such catches didn't catch up with me. They did.

The travel—and expense. The long distance calls

—and expense, etc. The regularity with which my salary hitherto had been handed over to me gave way to a distressing hit-or-miss prosperity.

On the other hand I did enjoy my new freedom. Instead of going to the city every day and having to journey across town and downtown and back in the evening, I somehow managed to take care of my "retainers" in two to three days, which were, of course, divided in mornings and afternoons. I learned to budget my time and to plan ahead.

It became apparent that designing on a free-lance basis was a considerably more serious business, but I found to my pleasure that my work became challenging and rarely routine. In much the same way as the customers picked me to do the job, I was able to be selective in my choice of customers and manuscripts. I acquired far more technical knowledge because I dealt with different manufacturers and problems. Being an independent designer, I could require quality in manufacture. Before, I had had little right to ask for better composition, presswork, or binding, because I was working for the manufacturer.

Working for manufacturers, I came in contact with a great number of publishers. My services were free to them and were absorbed by the manufacturer with his general overhead, or, perhaps, they were charged to the composing room operation. This work enabled me to understand the requirements of conservative publishers as well as of those who were dedicated to more experimental design. When I became a free lance the production managers of publishing houses dealing with me turned over to me more and more of their complicated manuscripts, manuscripts which required more experience and ingenuity than had been expected of me in earlier years. I worked harder and longer hours, I enjoyed the work more and I was paid more. I began to concentrate on production as I realized how much in demand this skill was and would be as production prices kept on spiralling higher.

A successful free lance will engage here and there in the production of books for a customer. This is one of the more profitable sides of free-lance work and has many interesting and enlightening facets. I tried to keep up with the technological innovations and—with the unkept promises. I learned that no matter what size, what type of production, what kind of design, a book remained a book. This has not only kept me as enthusiastic as I was when I first worked in the art department of a large book manufacturing concern but it gave me comfort whenever I needed it, which was often, indeed.

Even more than twenty years ago an attractive young lady, production manager of a small house, inquired if we could print by a new method the name of which momentarily escaped her. I replied yes, feeling my firm could always farm such a job out, if

necessary. Was it Offset? No? Gravure? No? Maybe
Silk-Screen? Collotype?

"No," said she, "something to do with a-a-oh yes,
'Letter'." "Letterpress?" I replied with some skepti-
cism "Yes," came the answer, "that's it!"

It is often reasoned that one has to be mad to be in
publishing or printing and that probably goes for
designing, too. But one is never bored.

Everything and everybody is there in this world of
mine: the people; the manuscripts and the finished
books; the skids of paper; rolls of bookcloth, and the
smell of printer's ink. The glossy photographs, the
type books, the pica rulers, and the slow, slow messengers, the crises, the "conferences," and the artwork covered by fresh tracing paper. Everything is
there or will be—how could one live without it?

As a nine-year-old boy I first played with a rubber
type set. Later came the little 3" x 4" press with real
printer's ink. Years of studies, jobs passed by, with
me as "ultimate consumer."

During the Depression it was probably not unusual to make your own printing press out of an old
screwtop copy press—which came via a junk shop
from an old office. I even printed with a homemade
wooden rotary press which did a nice job with linoleum. A six- to eight-color poster done in this manner was not unusual and I suppose it was a fore-
runner of the silk-screen process. Finally I lived with,

and virtually *in*, a job shop setting type and printing on a 17" x 22" Chandler & Price. After this I graduated to the white collar of design and production. There were all the type faces you could dream of, lots of different kinds of paper and more. Actually the restrictions proved to be far more severe, technical ingenuity was not required anymore (a forward attitude in design was stifled). Of necessity, I developed a more realistic attitude toward "commercial" quality. Still all was not lost. I learned to satisfy many different tastes. Sometimes I regret not being firm—or being able to be firm—with my clients. I am happy however to have designed so many different types of books for so many different types of publishers. I have even enjoyed designing manuscripts which I couldn't possibly understand.

Some time ago I met an old-world craftsman who makes leather handbags and belts and who showed me some beautiful skins from which he makes his wares. He smiled and said: "I like *Leder!*" Well, I guess I like books. . .

A book is a thing of beauty. True, there are many motives for writing it. Some are fine, such as sharing knowledge, experiences, and enthusiasm. Some authors must write stories out of their systems, and of course there are the hacks and paid scribes whose drivel has but one merit—"It sells!" To be involved in giving physical shape to books is a wonderful activity, perhaps being akin to playing or conducting the music composed by someone else. It is not unreasonable to expect a book designer to take his task seriously, to give it all his skill and love for the printed word, but not to be carried away by the possibilities of a typographic performance, a cadenza, as it were. What the designer feels is not always the same as what the publisher is willing to give to the book. Nor is the author always able to understand what the designer is trying to do (for him).

When the trio is in harmony, much can be done. If the designer falls in love with the book, as Pygmalion with Galatea, this book will become part of him. Having read as much of the manuscript as is available, or as much as interests him, he will proceed to plan a format in keeping with aesthetic and technical requirements of the manuscript. Such a format grows slowly or relatively fast even under the inevitable pressure that is generally supplied gratuitously.

This designer being stationed in his own studio likes to listen to classical music while working. I am not adverse to friendly interruptions such as requests for assistance with homework, listening to the practicing of one musical instrument or another, or even tasting half-finished dishes.

Just as conductors, sometimes, members of the orchestra, always, read the musical score—perhaps for the hundredth time—while playing it, so I have to refresh my typographic memory often (not always).

I do so mainly for accuracy in sizes. Of course, I am proud if I can sketch type in such a manner that it can be easily recognized for its characteristics and size.

If the publisher or editor turns over a complete or almost complete manuscript to me, I will oblige and design all of it at one time, to establish a uniformity of design—the absence of which can prove to be very disturbing.

Occasionally my best work has been produced by more or less painful cooperative effort. Working for myself, I have become involved often with authors and editors for considerably longer periods of time than I could have given them when I was with a manufacturer. I will gladly admit that a professional can sometimes be stimulated by the approach of a non-professional. With tact on both sides, very good results can be achieved, and a designer who is flexible will not be worse off for this experience. Frequently, of course, this "help" constitutes interference and the results can range from mildly disappointing to devastating. A good half of all authors who get into the act and who are allowed by the publishers to make demands in regard to the design or some phase of production can be a serious menace to the health and wealth of the publishers. They have "ideas" when it comes to the design of the book and/or the jacket. They sometimes feel their book should be printed in much the manner of a limited edition.

Worst of all they often have "a dear friend" who has thought of different ways of improving the book's physical features.

(It is true that many publishers counter this by changing the book's editorial content so radically that the author in turn wonders why *he* started to write the book in the first place.) Most authors of this type will not be satisfied with less than complete surrender, but I found that a fair proportion can be taken care of by offering to have their signature stamped in gold on the front cover.

No amount of knot cutting will help the poor fellow who gets caught in the nets of an advertising agency or who sells himself to a one-shot, self-made, author-publisher in the hope of a better fee for design and/or production. This "greater financial" reward is more than off-set by the heartbreaking drama of delay and speed-up, change after change of copy, changing from one manufacturer to another, or from material to material, to say nothing of the design. Why did they come to you in the first place, if they know everything better?

Strangely, designers are not expected to aid authors and editors with the factual knowledge that they may have, yet authors and sometimes editors, are natural-born designers. The fact that nearly everyone except the bookkeepers in publishing houses knows how to design, certainly adds action, excitement, and oh well, a little confusion to the job of turning a briefcase full of yellow paper and illustrations into a book.

Working with authors and editors takes time, but the result can be very gratifying, and I for one have never enjoyed compliments for my work more than when people indicated how appropriate they thought my design was.

The praise that I like best is when someone says of me, "He is very realistic." Well, we all have to be, and many of us are more or less realistic about our work.

Resisting those who in one way or another would ruin a good job is as important as artistic integrity.

To sum up, the conductor's own interpretation of the composer's work is what counts, but he must work with the material on hand, that is, with the musicians in his orchestra. He will want to please himself, and I think that this will please the audience and possibly also the critics. He must also please the members of the board of directors who don't always know too much about music and conducting. There may be technical limitations, too, such as the quality of the musicians and the number of rehearsals allowed.

When an architect undertakes to design a house, he generally must please his client, but he must also know what the needs of his client are and how much money can be spent on the construction of the building. For this reason, an architect must be familiar with all that contractors know, with the variety and cost of materials and equipment. Here, too, some compromises must be made. Here, too, integrity must be maintained.

It would seem therefore, that a book designer may, after all, not only have to be a typographer (printer) but also a conductor and an architect. Perhaps it would be best to be one of those Chinese jugglers one used to see in vaudeville balancing himself on a ball, juggling clubs or burning torches or hoops, and keeping a plate revolving on a stick on his forehead. That illustration will be recognized by many old hands at designing books, but it takes a number of years to become an old hand at juggling or book designing or what-have-you. It takes a bookcase full of books designed by you, innumerable crises weathered through, luncheons and dinners attended, lectures listened to, columns read, and plant visits made.

Once we have pleased publishers and authors, what can we do for printers and binders? What they want most, of course, are orders *when* they want them. *Accurate* composition, printing, and binding instructions come next in line and last, but not least, a tendency to pay bills *promptly*.

Very rarely does anyone toy with the idea of pleasing designers, so all I can suggest to that part of my audience who belong in this category is to try to please themselves. Start out by designing the way you think it should be done; it will be changed anyway!

Many publishers would like to know what constitutes a fair fee for the designing of most books done by a free lance. Many a designer would like to know, too. How is it possible to anticipate what the design of a book, particularly a textbook, an art book or a special project, will involve in knowledge, time, and aggravation? Publishers may try to pay as little, and designers charge as much as possible. But when fair-minded designers meet fair-minded production people, they can agree on a fair price.

However, it is wise to be very clear on what is expected of the designer. In addition to taking part in preliminary discussions about the book and preparing sample pages, sample bindings, and the actual layouts, a designer can be reasonably expected to provide detailed specifications which are an essential tool in the preparation and production of all books, particularly complicated or complex books.

The other day I struggled with the (for me) age-old problem of folding a 64-page sheet accurately. Finally, my assistant had to take over and she puzzled it out neatly. Just the day before, I had looked at a group of books on the desk of a production manager and discovered a copy cased-in upside down. "Save this one," I advised her, " it will be valuable!" In return, she handed me another copy of the same title from the little stack on her desk and said, "Look at these pages." I did and was not surprised to see page 60 follow 47, then 61 backed by 62 followed by 58, 48, and 49! Now that will really make a rare copy of a very dull book. Oh, the mysteries of imposition. Just one of the many things I never learned, although I should have.

Occasionally I visit a successful book agent who conducts his business from a two-room office with the help of a capable secretary. There are, of course, many bookshelves in his offices, also a few desks and I believe, four, or at the most five chairs. Needless to say three of them are piled high with books and manuscripts! There is space for a couple of telephones and for a typewriter, for a cup or two of coffee, and even for an elbow or two. The rest is reserved for books and, I fear, for the dust and soot which is the trademark of New York. When visitors arrive, a chair has to be hastily cleaned off, its quota of books will then perch precariously on top of still another pile.

All of this came to mind when I realized the other day that we at home just don't have enough chairs for such an operation. Not that I want to become an agent, but having temporarily switched my studio activities to the dining room table, I loaded it with manuscripts, galley proofs, materials, type books, and many other paraphernalia only to find out that I was expected to vacate this comfortable working space in favor of dishes, glasses, silverware, and in good time, a hot dinner. Our broad hearth proved a refuge—again temporarily. Perhaps a fire might be had in the fireplace and then where would we go, pencils, rulers, and all? In the confusion of moving some twenty or thirty pounds of assorted papers, a small seemingly insignificant piece of paper was misplaced. After frantic searches conducted by me and considerably more relaxed hunts on the part of my family, the innocent litle piece of paper turned up just about twenty-four hours later between two books. Still, no one here would believe what I would have had to go through to replace it.

Years ago before the advent of air conditioning, my office on the fourth floor of a large office building drew its supply of fresh air from a powerful fan. It was one of those humid summer days perhaps suitable to the tropics, shorts, drinks, but not conducive to book design. My title page was a product both of despair and of perspiration! The manuscript onion-skin stuck to my hands and forearms, so I opened all windows wide. By the time I could turn off the fan, the first three chapters were on the way to the street. The passers-by were very helpful. I managed to retrieve all or most of it. To this day I don't know if there were a few pages missing in some book causing raised eyebrows and despair to the author. As most of us amateur psychologists would say, I blotted out the title of the manuscript from my memory!

The book industry is highly individualistic, and frequently places emphasis on quality. There is opportunity for those who would create a book that is a pleasure to read. There are many people in "the industry" who will share their knowledge and not merely store it away for further personal use. It is surprising how much one learns all the time in one regard or another. But you will also find out how different plants operate, who can be counted upon, and who cannot. Naturally, this is very true of quality, with which one gradually becomes familiar, as it applies to printers, engravers and, for that matter, designers, copy editors, and indexers.

When your TV repair man is asked if he can repair radios he says "no." If you press him for the name and address of someone who can, he still says no. Now I don't mean to be a walking directory but I am being asked such questions all the time. True, I have recommended many people and have sometimes been very sorry. The same publisher who may have been happy to utilize my experience with certain specialists may blame me if anything goes wrong.

So I am not guaranteeing anyone anymore!

There are probably fewer people with or without a college education who gravitate toward books. Madison Avenue is the most popular goal today and it is more likely to supply status and the wherewithal to purchase it. But to those who have committed themselves to the book, a warning!

Not only is it unlikely that they may be able to switch halfway through their career to advertising or the like, but if they can make such a change they will find it difficult and painful. True, salaries are much higher, but the demands made upon the time and integrity of the members of that industry are also higher, often severely so. The customer is *always* right and must be served. With a noble exception or two, I have always worked *with* my employers in the book industry and not *for* or *under*. The more valuable your background is to your employer the more respect you may command.

By today's standards the rewards are not high. But no one will ever complain that his life "in books" has been dull.

HIJ

Part Three: Some Principles of Design

KL

The nineteenth century

and its industrial revolution produced more books than ever before, but less attractive ones. The printers became plant owners, and the foremen of their composition rooms and printshops were skilled workers, not artists or intellectuals. It was at the turn of the century and in the first quarter of the 20th century that the revival of fine old styles took place in industrial design—and books began to follow the trend.

It is to the credit of a number of designers, D. B. Updike, Bruce Rogers and others in the U.S.A., Stanley Morison and Francis Meynell among others in England, and still others in Germany and France, that modern book design as an art came into its own. Most of these men were printers who designed their own work, taking this part of the job away from the foreman—and thus establishing the function of the book designer as a separate one.

For more than 500 years, every book that was printed had to be designed in one sense or another. Master printers during the first 350 years of the craft designed and produced their own type and used it according to their own taste. A half-dozen major typographical eras have produced many great printers whose work was and still is identifiable.

More titles are produced by American publishers every year. More designers are employed by American publishers. Yet, I believe, many designers work on fewer books per year than they used to. Twenty-five years ago it was not unusual for one designer to be responsible for the entire output of a medium-sized house. Larger publishers indulged in the luxury of employing different designers for their trade and textbook departments. Some work was done—particularly for the very small publishers—by designers supplied at no cost by the large book manufacturers. There existed no more than a handful of free-lance book designers. Today there are multitudes of designers, many of them fresh from some school of graphics and in need of technical experience.

Meanwhile, there is a growing awareness within the publishing industry that most books should be designed by professionals.

Formerly, a manuscript was either turned over to one particular person or else given only very little typographical consideration; now it may go to any one of several different people—a designer in the house or at the manufacturing plant, or a free lance, and the work may eventually involve several dozen persons. Individuality has given way to expediency.

Whether one man is designing for twelve publishers or twelve designers are working for one publisher, I believe sincerely that the most important thing in designing is to serve the spirit of the manuscript.

It is hard to believe that a product such as a printed book can be handled in so many different ways. Practically all designers, publishers, and typesetters have varying systems of handling the manuscript. But when a manuscript has finally found its way to the desk of the designer—and it has been a long, tedious route—the production department of a publishing house is expected by everyone else to perform miracles, which means to get the manuscript designed immediately, set with no delays, and printed and bound into a salable book in time for whatever publication date is taken out of an imaginary hat by the sales and promotion people. The men and women in production departments would be surprised if this were not so. In fact, they would feel uncomfortable not being under some pressure.

In basic terms, most books consist of three parts: the text, the front (and back) matter, and the binding. The jacket should be a fourth integral part but as we all know, the sales department may have other plans than the designer or the editor or the production manager. Sometimes a "package" is successfully completed singly; more often the efforts of at least two people go into a book. Regardless of the number of design elements he controls, there is no question that the text deserves all the skill and interest of the designer. Only when he has solved any and all problems of the text properly may he proceed to the design of other parts of the book.

To design is also to designate. Designating or specifying type is one of the most important functions of the designer. It is here that he combines his aesthetic talent with his technical skill. It is also the one function which absorbs most of the designer's time. When he is ready to specify type for a manuscript, the designer must open the printer's type specimen books to see what typographical material is available.

A book type face should not call attention to itself. The designer must always keep in mind that his own tastes, and mere decorative effect are less important to the selection of a type face than the reader's ease of reading.

A book plant of average size has literally hundreds of type faces in different sizes. Some of these are suitable for book composition, some are not. In general, the designer has a great choice of machine faces to set the text in, and handset faces for title pages, chapter openings, etc.

Publishers don't usually work with one printer, or, for that matter, with a great number of printers. It is rare indeed when the production of books is entrusted to more than a handful of different printers. This, of course, depends a great deal on the quantity of books published and printed during a year.

Some of the book manufacturers, rather than issue type specimen books showing the type they have in their composing rooms, merely provide lists of type available, knowing that the publishers and the designers are acquainted with the major type faces and, if necessary, can obtain showings easily enough.

There are three kinds of type shops: first, the composing rooms that are part of a book manufacturer's plant; then, individual composing rooms that operate independently from printers and binders; and finally, the so-called type houses, which work mainly for the advertising industry and whose machine composition is usually too expensive for the book industry. However, the type houses carry display type in such abundance that when the publisher wants reproduction proofs for the preparation of the book printed by offset, their work is preferred, as it is done most skillfully. Publishers will also buy from them composition for children's books, as these books are short and need to be done well. The advertising industry has set high standards for composition and can afford to pay higher prices than the publishing industry can. The type houses, too, have available for the use of their customers, type samples and, of course, the type foundries supply very accurate and detailed type specimen books.

Occasionally, books are sent to a certain composing room because it has the particular type face which the designer wants to use. More often it works the other way around. Books are sent to typesetters or manufacturers for technical or economical reasons, and the designer has to satisfy himself with what is available.

The designer may have a preference for a certain type face or type faces for the book he is designing and try to make it conform with the figures he has worked out by casting off the manuscript. In other cases, he will cast off the manuscript first and determine how many characters per page he will require to set the book in a typographically sound style, making the right number of pages. In making such decisions and, depending on the size of the book, the designer will work mainly with type ranging from 8 to 12 point, which can be varied further by leading from as little as none to as much as several points. The measure and the number of lines per page will also vary with the trim size, so there is nothing left to do now but to decide on a suitable type face. The choice of such a type face is highly individual and should not be subject to deep considerations of style or the period of the manuscript.

The choice of type faces is magnificent, but also bewildering. Has it always been so? Indeed not, for Gutenberg's first alphabet cast in lead was of a size designed to reproduce the quill strokes of the scribes.

Every printer in the 15th century designed and produced all the type necessary for his print shop by himself. Naturally, he couldn't or wouldn't make great efforts to reproduce a variety of type faces. So these early printers had no problems in regard to the choice of type. They simply used what they had. How different it is today!

Within one hundred years of the invention of movable type, type foundries capable of producing a great variety of type were built and the multitude of printers by then in business, enterprising but less inventive and resourceful than those of the middle 15th century, were able to purchase type as they required it. By this time, too, new styles of type faces were designed and produced, specifically in Italy, and from that time on, to this day, new type faces in all sizes and for various uses have been developed everywhere.

In the 19th century, typesetting machines were invented in order to keep up with the rising demand of printing, and so far our own century has added cold composition to hot composition. Furthermore, computers are being utilized to speed up composition, sometimes at an astonishing rate of speed. We also use typesetting machines on which display faces —and sizes—are set to avoid wearing out display type, which is delicate and costly and occupies a lot of storage space in small shops.

Some of the more complicated textbooks, specifically mathematics, physics, and chemistry texts are set on the Monotype, the typesetting machine that sets letters individually.

When the designer has decided upon the selection of a type face, and when he knows definitely that his selection has been approved by the publisher, and that it is available at the printer, he must set out to deal with the intricacies of the manuscript.

Depending on whether it is a trade book, textbook, or a technical book, which may require specific handling of type, there are many components which must be properly understood.

Aside from the text proper, there may be a quantity of extracts of one nature or another as well as footnotes. In addition to that, we find part numbers and part titles, chapter numbers and chapter titles, and a variety of subheads. In textbooks of a technical nature there are diagrams, tables, and listings. These require very careful study in order not to emphasize them too much or too little.

To begin with, the designer must be certain what sizes of the type face he has chosen are available at the printer. It is surprising how often some sizes of certain type faces are just not available. Since a textbook frequently needs the entire range of sizes, it is wise to make doubly certain before specifying type, as missing type sizes can be obtained by the printer. Let us assume that the text of the book is set in 11 point. Then the extracts might be set in 10 or 9 point; and the footnotes and the index in 8 point.

Aside from the important headings in front matter and part titles, the range in a single type face from 14 down to 8 point offers a great variety of Roman caps, italic caps, upper and lower Roman, upper and lower italic, and small caps. In effect, over two dozen different possibilities are available. However, the reader can't be expected to identify such minute differences as 11 point or 10 point in one line, or 12 point small caps or 8 point caps. Therefore, the designer should limit himself to a much smaller variety of clearly contrasting type faces and type sizes. A skilled typographer can also blend successfully a small variety of entirely different type sizes.

It is tempting, of course, to use handset display type for chapter titles, as well as the front matter and some twenty or so lines will usually be absorbed in the costs. But, for example, in many textbooks, where there are many section titles, it becomes essential to set them on the machine. Actually, this may not be cheaper, but it is much more practical and less time-consuming than setting hand type, of which the printer may not have enough.

In the preparation of mechanicals for offset, the use of display type is easy enough, although by no means inexpensive. It is, therefore, essential for the designer to know which books are going to be printed by letterpress and which by offset.

It is my personal hope to make all books—not only the difficult textbooks—as readable as possible, and it is my theory that heads and subheads can be simplified. We may not need a large variety of different sizes and weights and faces, nor an ever-increasing number of indentations. I fear very much that outside of the law courts and the customs offices, very few people can make head or tail out of myriad subheads.

A manuscript travels from author to editor, to designer, to printer. The machine operator is expected to produce accurate composition at a steady clip. For this purpose, everything in the manuscript must be properly marked. The last link between the operator and the publisher is the foreman of the composing room. He, or someone he delegates, must mark up the manuscript for the operator. Most typesetters today prefer to do this rather than to receive manuscripts improperly or partially marked up by the publisher.

Where does the designer come in on this operation? I have frequently stated that the designer must combine talent and technical skill. However, the technical side of typography must not take an inordinate amount of time. After all, the designer must also have the pleasure of creating.

If the production department in the publishing house has personnel capable of handling manuscripts, they will usually do it expertly. The big question is then, who should do this job? Publisher, designer, or printer?

The editor can draw to the attention of the designer all that is important in the manuscript which should be brought to the attention of the printer. I believe it is the function of the editor, who is, after all, most familiar with the manuscript, to note these matters, and it is naturally the function of the designer to specify the typographic treatment. If the designer can take the time to mark up an entire manuscript properly, he will save the printer some trouble and time. The better this is done, the less likelihood of unnecessary author's alterations, which the publisher usually pays for.

So far I have not mentioned a device which is used by publishers and printers, and which tends to place all responsibility on the designer. This is the composition order; for short, "comp order." It can be excellent unless it becomes too complicated. When such an order has been designed to include every contingency under the sun, it tends to become very confusing. The designer must fill out every item, and there can be many. Usually the rules on the form are set so closely that it is physically difficult to cram in all the information. Four or five duplicate copies do not make the job any easier.

Proofreading, of course, is usually done in the print shop, and also by the author or editor. But in some cases an extra or "final" reader is employed.

He does not read against copy as the other two do, but he reads for content, accuracy, and consistency. He can often make very valuable suggestions which might have been overlooked by people directly involved in mechanical proofreading.

An accurate and detailed sample page is a necessity, and it helps everyone concerned a great deal more than the scribbles on pink, yellow, or blue "comp order" sheets.

Sample pages have existed as long as there have been commercial printers. However, their shapes have been changed considerably through the years. In very old type specimen books we find not only similar set pages in different sizes (type, measure, depth of page) as in some of our contemporary type books, but a great variety of page sizes as demonstrated by the simple expedient of varying margins around the printed page. The page sizes in those days had names such as quarto, octavo, duodecimo, indicating the number of pages which were obtained by folding one mould-made sheet.

Modern production methods, particularly those of the paper industry, have made page size limitations merely a matter of economics. To be sure, the more choice we have in papers, paper sizes, printing processes or for that matter, binding materials, the less we are inclined to use them. A new trend has been established, restricting all these choices so as to produce efficiency—meaning, of course, dollars and

cents. (This is no place to quarrel with that, and I am happy to report that not everyone believes in this dogma of standardization.)

In line with the great speed requested of the designer and typesetter, sample pages are often not requested or are simply ignored. It is quite true that they take time to produce, as they are usually set and proofread quite carefully, printed on a proof press and hand folded, and they cost more money than most of us like to admit.

But consider what such a sample page can do. It can be shown to the author, if the publisher's representative, whoever he might be, has a strong will or is empowered to take this chance. Some authors are immensely pleased to see a page of their work in print quickly, others have their own ideas on typography or else they have advisors who do.

The sales and publicity departments naturally can use sample pages for their own purposes, although they usually prefer to work with jackets. How a well-functioning production department can manage without the sample page I don't know. In the course of the months following the day when the manuscript is turned over to the printer, there will be many times when a reference to a printed sample page will save time, money and aggravation, maintain good will, and create better looking books.

The designer naturally expects to see a sample page, although it is his business to have enough imagination not to require one. But it is nice to justify your typographic instincts, particularly when you don't have enough time to look at the type book and check just what 16-point Bulmer looks like.

Editors may not feel any need for sample pages, but they somehow seem to refer to them, even for trade books. Textbook editors would have a very hard time indeed working without sample pages. In some cases meticulous textbook editors, working with designers and production managers and with cooperative authors, may go through a whole series of sample pages showing every possible head, subhead, type of table, caption, etc., until they are quite certain that everybody is satisfied. Such a series of sample pages will cost hundreds of dollars but is bound to save many thousands of dollars, avoiding massive costs in resetting or repaging.

Now to the physical aspects of a sample page. At one time, in the 1930's, a manufacturer might produce a sample page, but another manufacturer might get the job, perhaps because the latter could underbid by a few cents. In general this hasn't changed, but it did produce an awful lot of sample pages, sometimes for the same book. In that period some printers, knowing quite well that they would probably not get the job, set as little as possible and it was not unusual to find sample pages without the title of the book or the name of the printer, or for that matter, with nothing resembling a "spec" page.

The sample pages that did contain all necessary information usually began with a chapter opening, showed two facing pages of straight text, and wound up with a specifications page. In the case of a trade book, there is really no reason to have much more unless typographical problems in the book need to be worked out promptly. In the early years, during and after the Depression, some publishers were not satisfied with a mere four pages, but requested a 16-page signature which was produced in large quantities to be used by salesmen and sometimes were even bound into a "dummy."

I have stated before that there is nothing so trivial in a complicated book that it need not be set in a sample page. Naturally, different books present different problems. It is most advisable to solve as many as possible immediately.

I do not suggest the setting and printing of complicated front matter unless, of course, one can be reasonably sure that the setting remains as designed. The reason for that is, even after sample pages have been set, one can change from one type face to another. Sometimes technical circumstances make that mandatory. When this happens it is usually a waste of time and money to have a complete set of front matter, as a different type face will not only mean different type for the front matter, including the title page, but it could conceivably mean a very different design approach. I am not happy about the practice of starting composition, or even "going into pages," and letting sample pages be set meanwhile. Ten to one, something is going to go wrong or at least someone is going to be very unhappy.

Even in a very simple sample page it is essential to be meticulous about such things as space. The designer—and I am no exception—naïvely assumes that the printer will interpret his layouts down to even one point of space. One easily forgets that two people can see just such a fine nuance differently, and that if the type is not drawn or traced accurately, the space between lines will be inaccurate, too.

Even while I am writing this, I remember two experiences with sample pages worth repeating: In the first case I was gently persuaded, in order to expedite the job, not to bother with a sample page and I was assured that nothing would go wrong and any immediate changes would be cheerfully made. Needless to say, no time was saved, substantial errors were committed; subsequently compromises were made and some disappointment was created for all concerned.

On the sunnier side of this ledger, I had a telephone call from a young editor who had spotted what she thought might be an error of judgment on my part. I had not then received the sample page, and it is quite possible that I might not have noticed this error, not having the entire manuscript on my desk. She, on the other hand, had the use of the manuscript, compared it with the sample pages and came up with an improvement for which I was very grateful.

The type or types of paper to be used in a book must be considered along with the styles and sizes of type. Books have been written on the history of paper. I cannot and would not compete with them, but I would like to mention that the advent of substantial printing machinery in the early part of the 19th century created an ever-increasing, almost momentous demand for large-size sheets of book paper. We say "book paper" because in its properties and qualities it usually is different from writing paper or wrapping paper or from thousands of kinds of papers that are in use today. It has to be of a lasting quality. It has to be suitable for various printing processes. This means that printing ink must be absorbed by the paper fibers and dry reasonably soon. Different types of printing require different sheets of paper. To print illustrations properly, various papers have to be used.

The 19th century saw the building of many paper mills. Paper became a great industry in this country as well as in Europe. Canada and Scandinavia provided the great quantity of wood pulp needed for the making of less expensive paper in quantity. The days of ragpickers were numbered. To be sure. we still make rag papers with a content of from 25 percent to 100 percent, but they are used for bank notes, legal documents, insurance policies, and fine stationery. Only occasionally do we use them for book work.

Paper mills have always been dependent on three raw material sources—wood, water, and power—and have usually located themselves within close proximity to all three. In the past, as legend will have it, wood supplies would become exhausted, requiring the mill to pack up and move on. Today, no mill could possibly be moved economically, and in order to insure a sufficient supply of wood pulp, the wood farmers are taught to plant two or three seedlings for every tree that they cut. In this way a continuous supply is made available, and the income of the farmer is assured.

The events that took place in the Dust Bowl during the Great Depression, and the experience of Spain, for another example, have shown the enormous danger of deforestation.

Even so, American paper mills are running 24 hours a day, seven days a week, and for that reason large quantities of chemically cooked and bleached wood pulp is imported, primarily from wood-rich countries such as Canada and Sweden.

Quite naturally, the size of printing paper is dictated by the printing surface of a printing press. Newer, bigger, and faster presses have been introduced successively during the past 150 years. Meanwhile, in addition to letterpress printing, lithography and gravure were developed for commercial use. Both have necessitated the preparation of paper stock specifically for these processes.

It is likely that one could find literally hundreds of trim sizes. Formerly, certain book sizes such as "quarto, octavo, duodecimo" were dictated by folding a standard size sheet into four, eight or twelve pages, etc. These sheets were "mould-made" papers; that is, papers that were usually made with a mould as big as two men could handle. The paper machines, increasing in size throughout the 19th century, made a continuous roll of much less expensive paper which had to be cut apart or "sheeted."

Modern sheet sizes are measured in inches. For example, a 25x38 inch sheet is a multiple of 6x9 inches and would make thirty-two pages when folded, allowing ⅛ inch to be trimmed off at the top, outside, and bottom. A related measure is basis weight, the weight (depending on bulk and density) of one ream, or 500 sheets, of the basic size of 25x38 inches.

As we well know, the paper needs of publishing houses differ sharply. The larger firms have established their individual systems which, usually, they administer expertly. What paper stock is needed by a small to medium size publishing house? Naturally, it depends on the type of books they publish. Paperbacks require as inexpensive a sheet as possible.

However, great efforts should be made to obtain a pleasant white sheet, even if it is an inexpensive wood pulp stock. We cannot here go into the technique of paper production such as the cost of fillers, sizing, or coloring, except to say that paper made on machines has a grain running in the same direction as that of the flow of paper on the machine. Although the grain of the sheet used is frequently governed by the printing process or the complexity of the copy, it should always be considered in the light of its influence on folding and binding. An art book requires almost the very opposite in ingredients and in price range from the stock used for paperbacks. Regular trade books and long illustrated textbooks require a variety of stock.

The paper industry supplies an astonishingly large quantity of different papers for different purposes. We will see presently why they are not all suitable for books.

In order to purchase paper at what we might call a standard price, no smaller quantity than 5,000 lbs. should be ordered. With average books requiring from ¾ to 2 lbs. of paper, usually the amount of paper ordered is at least 10,000 lbs. The lowest price available to the book industry is one that can be applied to "carload" orders. This amounts to 36,000 lbs. Even small publishers use many carloads a year and are entitled to a contract price from the supplier, usually a paper merchant.

Most paper merchants handle the products of several paper mills and deal with a great number of book publishers as well as with other paper users. This makes the supply of merchandise fairly flexible. Sometimes an order can be processed quickly by utilizing paper tentatively laid aside for someone else who, however, does not need it yet. Sometimes orders can be placed advantageously with paper mills that might not have received them directly. The paper merchant and, in particular, the salesmen who service your account are of the greatest importance to you. A good paper salesman will check out important points with you that you might not be aware of, such as the direction of the grain, sizing of the paper for offset, trimming four sides, "skidding" properly for the needs of your printer, and working out the most economic and expedient manner of shipping the stock. It is very advisable to find out from your printer, before you order any paper, whether the stock you have in mind suits him and, of course, which way the grain is to run. Because of some experiences years ago, I have never ordered paper for offset or gravure without discussing it with a printer. Some stock that works very well for printer A may not work for printer B. It is a very unhappy experience when the printer calls you to tell you that your book looks terrible, or worse yet, when he doesn't bother.

The friendly help that you can get from all paper

salesmen naturally does not mean that you must leave all decisions up to them. They give you, in effect, part of a very important course in paper. The rest of it you learn by frequent discussions with your manufacturers, by the actual needs of your firm, and by occasional visits to paper plants. I cannot emphasize enough the need to learn about paper all that can easily be learned in such a way. Often a degree of ignorance in these matters is not only costly, but in fact, *very* costly.

Figuring out quantity, spoilage in presswork and binding, price, and schedule is often tedious. Publishers naturally have to order a great deal of different kinds of paper through the year, and there is no end to the computation of figures. Get help when you can, but don't depend on it.

There is no room here to state the many needs of various publishers. Ordering a large quantity of paper presents different problems from those in ordering a small quantity. You must have paper available not only for your immediate needs, but for those that you can schedule, not only for one printer, but for several with whom you deal. This, of course, means a large paper inventory, and you will probably have to have discussions about it with your treasurer.

When you need small quantities, less than a "making order," you will find that you cannot expect the same service from the supplier, and it is likely that terms will be a little stricter. While you probably cannot afford much of an inventory, you may have to be prepared for a smaller reprint than you had planned. This means that you must try to combine the need for paper for more than one title. It is true that one manuscript may be short and another long, that you may want to use papers of varying weights or bulks. You may have to make a compromise here. That, however, is not as difficult as it seems. The 55 lb. stock can serve such titles as would normally require either 50 or 60 lb. stock. The same is true of trim sizes.

If you are working on a substantial project, a book which requires a sizable quantity of paper, you can ask for just about anything in size, weight, or bulk. However, you must be prepared for reprinting quantities which do not require a making order. If you are reasonably certain of a reprint, whether you expect it to be small or large, you can, of course, order more stock in the first place. Such a reserve, however, needs to be stored somewhere and could be part of an inventory.

Paper is an unpredictable commodity. The paper mills and the paper merchants can tell you that different making orders of paper may vary—perhaps not in color, but possibly in weight—and also that a paper machine cannot be turned off like a faucet. This means that it is understood that your run of paper may be "short" or "long" by as much as 10 percent. Because the weight of the paper cannot be controlled to 100 percent accuracy, there exists a further unknown quantity. Thus, a 50 lb. stock may actually weigh 52 lbs., or possibly 48 lbs. In any case, when using sheets you will be charged for 50 lbs., which is what you ordered, but with many more books being produced on web or roll fed equipment another problem has been introduced. By obtaining a 48 lb. instead of a 50 lb. stock you will realize a few more signatures than you expected. A 52 lb. stock will do the opposite. The sizing of bulky paper for offset is not always successful and may present technical difficulties to the printer, particularly where illustrations are concerned. This is but a small list of problems which may arise.

The keeping of paper inventory is not easy but absolutely necessary. Because you must have paper to print books on, and because you cannot pick up quantities of paper overnight, you must always be aware of what quantity of this precious commodity you have on hand. A paper inventory can be a handful of filing cards held together by a rubber band, but it can also be considerably more intricate. It depends entirely on the experience and the personal wishes of your production manager, and the number and variety of books you have to produce.

It is logical that the most important task in designing any book is to make it readable and attractive—in that order! This means, first of all, the text matter, then the headings and only then the front matter. Depending on circumstances, the front matter of a book comes to the designer with the manuscript—or else it doesn't. In the latter case a terse note appears somewhere on whatever constitutes the first page of the manuscript: front matter to come. Just *when,* you will not be able to find out. Perhaps the title is not final, the dedication has not been decided upon, the contents page has not been made up or, for that matter, it is not yet clear if there will be a list of illustrations. Once, when I inquired when and from where these would come, the production manager said with an evil smile, "*You* will make them up!"

But let us say all the front matter is in your hands and you are ready to design it.

If the type face for the book has been settled, and you know who will set the front matter, all you need to know is which type faces are available to you. No use setting your heart on something the printer must import from Italy or Switzerland.

In line with this I think some designers are not quite used to the idea that more books are printed by offset now (from the first edition on). I am not giving away any trade secrets if I say that for very little more money, designs for offset can be made that in letterpress are usually too costly. Repros obtained from typehouses offer far greater selections of display type.

Whether you have chosen a uniform type face for everything, or a contrasting display face, the face used for the major headings naturally will look equally correct on the title page. It is always wise to anticipate the entire typographical needs when the first chapter title is being designed. At this point a seemingly small matter ought not to be overlooked. Just as with type, there should be consistency in styling. That is to say, don't set chapter heads flush after a modern fashion and center all type on the title page in a traditional manner; or *vice versa*.

There is really no page in the entire front matter that is more important than the other. In a good book —I mean in a well-designed book—I feel there should be a quiet, attractive evenness. A title page to which the designer gave his all plus plenty of display, sticks out, alright—like a sore thumb! On the other hand it is sad to see a contents page or a dedication which has been designed with little thought or interest. I believe also that there should be an equal consistency of tone and color, which means that a quiet 14 point upper and lower-case chapter head will not blend with 60 point caps on the title page, no matter how short the title may be. For that matter, I don't see why part titles have to be as dramatic as a Wagnerian opera.

When double-spaced title pages are indicated—perhaps to incorporate a frontispiece or because there is a great deal of information that cannot fit easily on one page—a conventional layout for the book is out. One of the problems is to be aware of the amount of paper that will disappear between the facing pages of a double spread. If you wish to spread an illustration or map across both pages, *beware of what will not show!* If the title is broken in two, consider carefully how much word-space will disappear and what to do about it. Actually, it is wise to design your double spread in a book, not on flat paper, and then take the pages out of the book and plan the layout accordingly.

The half or bastard title should be an echo, or rather, an introduction to the title page. A 25 percent reduction in the size of the title or else a modest text-size cap or even small cap line will do well. Textbooks should have more prominent half titles than fiction and other trade books. This is an intuitive theory which also creates quickly recognizable binding designs for textbooks.

While we are discussing title pages, which, of course, should also be correlated or tied in with the binding design, it will not hurt to repeat again how important it is to allow the spirit of the book to show —its delicacy or its toughness, whatever its quality may be.

It is a jarring experience to find wild contrasts of artistic feeling displayed in the various components of a book. This can happen often enough when the art director orders a jacket in a style that hasn't anything to do with the typography of the inside of the book. If this is known to those who order "art," why does it happen so often? Perhaps the hapless art director cannot read all manuscripts or reprints; I think, though, *someone* should.

After the title page or pages, comes the C/R or copyright page. Publishers are pretty definite about what information they want on that page, but don't care much what the page looks like. This attitude is often found to apply to index or bibliography pages, too. Dedications are unhappily squeezed in somewhere on a copyright page. All of these pages deserve as much—well, *almost* as much—attention as the title page.

A copyright page can be very attractive if it is subdued but legible; a dedication page can and should be charming because it is—in a manner of speaking—a gift or a bouquet. Bibliography pages should be particularly legible to be useful. This rules out setting them very small to save a little space.

This is equally true of index pages. Attention should be devoted to the size of page references so they are at least legible. A little extra space-break can be inserted between alphabetical sections of the index.

A device I have found very helpful when books are illustrated, is to allow space for an occasional small illustration here and there to break the monotony of front matter and back matter (BM). This is particularly true where these sections are long and tedious and when the book is done by offset, as so many art books are.

When all FM and BM is done, it is a good idea to compare these pages, as some small inconsistencies may creep in which can still be easily repaired.

A designer does his best work if he is given adequate time to design the book and can prepare text, FM, and BM all at once. If, on the other hand, he is urged to "give us a chapter opening and a text page, so we can go right into pages," he will find it harder to produce the quality of design that is expected of him.

Although the designer rarely has exclusive control of the design of the jacket, a few, almost historical, facts about book jackets are soon apparent. Since the end of the first World War, jackets (dust wrappers at that time) have been used universally.

The earlier efforts consisted of big type—later large lettering—and the rest filled with a large halftone color illustration, possibly an idealized drawing. The use of color was sparing; offset did not yet exist. Everything became larger, book and all being painfully padded. Certainly no time for delicate jacket design . . . *Tempora mutantur.*

Eventually came the breakthrough. Airbrush calligraphy, fine sketches, offset printing. A generally more continental approach to jacket design imported by some enterprising publishers.

Then followed the four-color process full page halftone for historical novels, mostly complete with well-proportioned heroine in such a state of undress as public taste expected and condoned. With the advent of paperbacks, most of the dress vanished, the historical background, too. The titles were incidental and Western, crime, or sex novels were sold on the strength of a jacket that held out great promises to the less mature and immature reader.

What happened to the type jackets in all that time? Right along, university presses, for reasons of economy, and some continental and British publishers for even better reasons, had stayed with good typography, usually in two colors and often with a decorative box.

Now some American publishers realized that to compete with all that color work in dress or undress would require drastic measures. A few switched to black and white. It was new, refreshing—and cheaper. It could be prepared quickly, required no complicated process work, corrections, etc.

Slowly, as the "pocketbook" became a "paperback" assuming respectability, some of the best commercial artists became interested in this field and produced a great many wonderful designs. The very limitation of space available to them worked in their favor. In effect, they turned out little masterpieces, miniature posters as it were.

Eventually serious modern art was used, and such

painters as Ben Shahn were commissioned to design book jackets. More color was used than before. What next?

There are many ways in which a design can be put on paper. A beginner will probably be happiest tracing the type he has selected. This is, of course, time-consuming but it has the advantage of being accurate. That is to say, if it is done well, the layout will not only reproduce the character of the chosen type face but in height and length each word and the entire line will (or should) look like the real thing. With some experience you can create a striking resemblance to the type face you selected and with a little concentration you can copy a line of type the way it will look when printed. Actually there is nothing more attractive than an imaginative, neat sketch. Your eye and your hand both directed by your brain will create something more artistic than the best reproduction proof. Call it a design or a sketch, whatever, it is original. Of course, it isn't the function of printing to create originals, it is to duplicate identically. Therefore, you and you only have originally created something that the type and press cannot reproduce.

Whenever someone asks me what kind of paper I use for my layouts and what kind of pencils, I am embarrassed. It seems fussy and picayune to talk a great deal about such a detail. On the other hand there is no simple answer. Of course, I could say: "What do *you* use?"

If the layouts are intended to be filed away with specification pages, perhaps not to be looked at by anyone in the publishing house, that is one thing. Layouts to be submitted to the author, the editor, and the production manager plus a number of assistants, the presentation should look neat and attractive. In any case it is likely to be sent to the printer. There it will be handled not like a fragile antique, but as what it actually is—a set of visual directives for the printer.

Designers and layout men use basically two kinds of papers which are available in most art supply stores. The most common type used for this purpose is tracing paper, which comes in a variety of qualities. The best and most expensive quality is a fairly heavy sheet which is not too transparent and which, while it looks good and is pleasant to the touch, has an unfortunate property of being brittle. If it is folded, it will soon break. The thin grades of tracing paper, on the other hand, curl up at the merest suggestion of humidity. The best bet for the designer is a medium quality. There are so many kinds of tracing paper available that it is best for the designer to find out himself by trial and error what is most suited to his needs. I would most certainly advise anyone to stay away from sheets or rolls. I like a 9 x 12 inch pad best because it is easy to handle and most trim sizes will fit this size.

In the advertising industry or where tracing is not important, artists use a fairly light stock, more opaque than transparent. Because this paper is very white, a soft pencil, No. 1 or No. 2, will produce good black and white contrasts. If you put white paper under your tracing paper after you are finished, it will make your layout show up. Pads made from inexpensive new stock which are frequently used in art schools and in advertising are not suitable at all for book design. The stock is very soft, it breaks easily, and it looks very cheap.

The abrasive quality of tracing paper necessitates the use of very hard (5H or 6H) pencils. Using hard pencils makes it possible to trace delicate type accurately. The letters can be produced by working over the lettering with a HB pencil. When this is done, however, it pays to spray a small amount of clear fixative over the layout to prevent smudging. This will also protect it from getting soiled.

For people who do a lot of layouts, particularly under artificial light, it is recommended to use paper which is tinted slightly green. This will relieve the strain on your eyes. One place where such stock is available is the Cooper Union Art Supply Store in New York City.

The papers I have discussed so far are intended primarily for the handful of layouts needed for front matter, chapter openings, and special matter. If, as in the case of illustrated books, the designer has to lay out a great number of pages, it is customary to have special dummy pages. They are printed, usually by offset, by the printer who is to be involved in the project.

The artist proceeds to prepare a double spread layout by outlining the trim size of two facing pages, adding a second "Bleed" rule all around. This rule should be ⅛ inch from the inside box. He will, furthermore, indicate the center line as well as the column or columns of the type page overall (printed area), complete with lines showing where the running heads and folios go.

It is practical to show all measurements and margins as well as all other pertinent information, such as the title and the publisher's name, above the layout. All of this is done in black or red ink and should be printed in fairly light blue ink on a good quality of ledger or offset stock.

I prefer the use of some smooth, very white material and I like a good deal of extra margin to be around the layout. As these layouts will often have stats or galley proofs pasted on them, a poor quality of paper will make changes or repairs most difficult. In printing the layout sheets, a small overrun of perhaps 10 percent is advisable as errors or changes will occur. Single page corrections are not practical. The designer will prepare new facing page layouts.

Few designers collect religiously a copy of every book they have designed, and still fewer designers will hold on to the masses of sample pages and layouts they have produced. That is a shame, for after some years you would find old friends among them, as in old, long-forgotten letters, bundled and stowed away.

Some day I would like to see an exhibition of sketches both of typographic designs and of book jackets with special emphasis on rejected material. Such a show of the work of a variety of designers would tell an eloquent story. What a wealth of talent we would then discover! Layout materials are immensely useful in teaching, which any designer will do sooner or later—teaching a class or individual assistants. When I began designing I did not have time to collect everything. Later on I kept only the best. But now I feel sorry I didn't keep them all. It is worthwhile for any designer to take stock from time to time of his progress, and the development of his talent, skill and experience. No matter how modest a beginner is, or should be, he will, or should, strive to become a master in his craft.

Most layouts when they leave the desk of the designer are lost to him. The mails, the messengers, the desks, and files of the production department, the shops and waste bins of the printer will often dispose of them. For this reason it is good practice, even though it may mean extra effort, to produce and keep on file duplicates of your layouts and sketches.

At your request some publishers or printers may give you a Xerox print or photostat. If you know from experience that this cannot be done, you can make a rough tracing of your layout very rapidly. You hardly need rulers nor is it necessary to make the type look "pretty." There will be many times when you wished you'd done it.

Before typewriters, business letters were written in a certain ink and put between the pages of a thick ledger filled with blank pages of Bible paper. The book was then put in a press and, as pressure was applied, a duplicate of the letter was printed into the book. Thus this book, containing thousands of sheets, became the one and only file in the office. Perhaps it would be possible to keep a special tracing paper pad containing a record of the designer's layouts. It might be worth it.

Incompetent sales clerks are not likely to make a store popular, and a smelly restaurant does not establish an atmosphere of comfort and confidence in what foods are going to be served. In the same way, galley or page proofs can be the determining factor in a repeat sale of composition, or in fact, complete manufacturing.

Anyone who has ever been in a proofroom or who is familiar with the abundance of galleys or page proofs in the production department of a publishing house can readily understand that confusion cannot be far off. After all, these proofs look very much alike.

It takes a good hard look or two to identify the title or author or publisher.

What do we—authors, editors, designers—expect of proofs? Naturally, first of all, accuracy. Second, typographical quality which is actually more a matter of imaginative typographical design and skillful typesetting. Last but not least, the presentation of these proofs should be attractive and informative, and they should handle well.

Why not good proof paper? Let us start out with the material. Commonly printers use machine finish stock, usually a 40 or 50 lb. sheet. The size varies from shop to shop but doesn't usually go below 6½" x 21". Larger proofs of a better quality of paper would be most welcome to those who work with proofs. The only drawbacks are the greater weight and higher cost to the printer. Galley for galley, however, the weight is no factor, and in relation to composition and printing prices, the cost of proof paper is unimportant.

But what a pleasure it is to work with white, clean paper that doesn't get crumbled or messed up at the slightest provocation, a stock you can write on in ink or in pencil *and* erase without fear of tearing; a paper, furthermore, that can be pasted with rubber cement and removed reasonably without tearing.

Now for the informative side. How about clear-cut and readable information such as printer's name, publisher's name, title, first or revised proofs, name of linotype operator, date of composition, and last but not least, the galley number in large type, 24 point or more, at the top of the galley. This is information one needs whether one works with the first or 100th line of each galley.

Then there is also the human element, the author who wants to help. This is not unlike the toddler who helps Mother cooking or baking or is allowed to help wash the car—only the author usually thinks this up all by himself. Sometimes he writes corrections in longhand between the lines; sometimes he makes inserts quite professionally but forgets to supply them attached to the galley proof where the machine operator can see them; sometimes he uses the scissors and the glue pot.

Like an old fashioned journalist in shirt sleeves and visor, he cuts galleys apart and pastes them together again, sometimes—so help me—in an unending roll. If you ask him how the printer is to identify the type which has now moved several chapters ahead or back, he says very innocently, "Why, he *has* the type, hasn't he?"

On the other hand, I am happy to relate a story where a textbook publisher dealing with a complicated book consisting of text, notes, extracts, and footnotes had each proofed on a different color stock:

white for the text, rose for the editor's notes, blue for the extracts, and yellow for the footnotes. It was up to the editor, then, to cut them apart, identifying each carefully, and making a tidy paste-up of every page. It made life easy for the printer, the author, and the designer, and was well worth the extra effort.

Among my possessions are drawing boards, T-squares, sharp razor blades and a quantity of rubber cement and thinner. These possessions, unfortunately, have not given me the talent to produce the kind of "mechanicals" I could be proud of. For some reason which I have not been able to figure out, an extra one-sixteenth of an inch has usually found its way into one of the corners of my mechanicals. Furthermore, no matter what rulers I have used, or no matter what liquid to draw the rules, smudges occur. It takes extra time to retouch or erase them. In short, I have avoided making mechanicals except the most simple ones.

There are, of course, many designers, particularly young designers, who could do a good job on them. If they are employed in a large publishing house, chances are that they spend a considerable time doing just that. They must be very patient and very neat.

Large and small publishers often turn over design and mechanical assignments to services such as Libra Studio, New York, where they can let their worries change hands. Here, many production aspects of book design can be creatively handled to produce the best results.

Beri Greenwald of Libra has probably heard more sad stories, gone through more crises and fixed up more errors than even the much harassed production manager. Miss Greenwald worked in the art departments of advertising agencies before she opened her own studio and is thus familiar with the considerable numbers of production problems which seem to be part of the atmosphere of the graphic arts industry. When she began to specialize in book work, she may have felt that the world of books would be more easy-going than that of Madison Avenue. At any rate, she is calm, competent, and charming. All these qualities are a must for a young woman who deals with designers, production people and their assistants and secretaries, typehouses, photostat places, messengers, and printers.

Needless to say, among the many jobs in the house at any one time, some go through rapidly while others drag for a half year or more for varied reasons; each job reflects particular styles or work methods of designers or publishers; and each job has to conform to certain technical requirements of the various printers.

(At this point I ought to admit how many times my own instructions may have been hard to read or ambiguous or just non-existent. Perhaps other designers are better at writing instructions, but I refuse to believe that I am the only offender.)

To do a successful job of producing mechanicals, you must understand design—in this case, book design—have a good working knowledge of type faces, know printing processes, and always be patient with people.

One must hold the T-square straight, keep razor blades sharp, and not cut oneself. The consistency of rubber cement must be as uniform as the preparation of a fine sauce. Fresh reproduction proofs must not be smudged with fingers or grayed by rubber cement or cut into. A page folio must not be dropped inadvertently. Nothing is to be pasted upside down, and everything has to be aligned properly. If running heads or entire pages are not aligned properly, the fault had better lie with the folding machine than with the studio. Allowing any type or other important material to get too close to the trim line invites disaster, as the standard ⅛ inch "for trim" has been known to grow into 3/16 or even more.

Preparing mechanicals for the book industry goes back to the beginnings of offset printing at the time when offset was synonymous with "cheap and gray." It was usually the task of a poorly paid artist-worker in the print shop to lay out pages on light boxes, stripping the various parts of each page into position. In general, such pages consisted of text of which line negatives were supplied and of illustrations which were either line or halftone negatives. In addition, there might be miscellaneous lines of type. All of these were stripped together as negatives. In the end each negative page was imposed properly and put together with the rest of the form. This was preparatory to burning in the negatives on the printing plates.

More and more the printers discouraged this practice, either by raising their prices for this operation or by taking a great deal of time with it. It became necessary for the publisher to produce mechanicals which, in effect, were accurate layouts complete with all type and occasionally with Velox prints. If halftones were involved, red outlines were drawn on the mechanicals indicating exact position.

The standard procedure today is to prepare mechanicals in double spreads which will be photographed at the shop. Pages will then be imposed properly and stripped together on the light-table. Trim and bleed lines and register marks can now be painted out easily on the negative, and all that need to be stripped in, normally, are whatever halftones are required.

One of the first jobs Miss Greenwald did for me a number of years ago was paste-up of pages for a two-color book done for the American Management Association. The design problem was to reconcile a quantity of folders done in an unusually naïve manner for use in large plants. These folders had to be part of a book also containing new printing and a border printed in color, which was to make the little folders more palatable. Every page required the pasting of a frame bleeding on three or four sides, with headings, running heads, folios, and from one to three additional bits of copy. I believe the job entailed the pasting and alignment of close to 2000 pieces of paper.

Ever since then, I have designed all kinds of illustrated books, and Miss Greenwald has interpreted my scribbled directions and has bravely wielded razor blades and rubber cement brushes. The books have come out on time; the crises have been forgotten, and it has been fun!

MN

Part Four: Practical Aspects

OP

When a young designer

is first given an opportunity to design a book all by himself, he may find himself in one of two situations —that of "not rocking the boat" or, on the other hand, of trying to "make a big splash."

At one extreme, the powers that be may request the young designer merely to "follow the style" of one of the many books in the publisher's library. Or perhaps the designer is too timid to take chances, and chooses to "follow the style" anyway. Or a printer or his salesman may be asked to help the neophyte designer.

At the other extreme, the designer may be given no supervision and may simply be challenged to "take care of" the design himself. Perhaps, too, he may have some forceful ideas of his own. Perhaps he cannot believe that the printer's knowledge will be useful to him.

In either situation, it is practical experience that gives confidence—experience, one hopes, that will produce neither over-confidence nor boredom, and will leave the designer interested and enthusiastic about his job.

Never before in graphic history has there been such a variety of tools and materials available to designers. The first printers worked with one or two type faces. The present-day designer has a choice of hundreds of different text faces, each available in many sizes, and an equally large choice of display faces and sizes. There is a great variety of kinds, shades, surfaces, and sizes of paper—even though, in book design, we try to limit ourselves in the varieties of paper used. In binding techniques and materials, there is virtually no limitation other than that of economy.

How do we go about obtaining experience in the use of all these opportunities? Different people, obviously, acquire skill and experience in different ways and at different speeds. To start by "not rocking the boat" usually produces dull, disappointing results, if only because most copies are weaker than the originals. The cautious young designer will first study those books that seem to him "safe" typographically. He will notice that designers before him have shown preferences in sizes, in paper and in type faces. Perhaps he will go along with such preferences. Perhaps he will have other ideas. But after a brief time he will not, or at least he should not, simply go on copying other books.

I have always been fascinated by the story that

handwriting tells about a person. Our handwriting, beginning in school, evolves gradually, and finally, in adult life, becomes more or less fixed. Perhaps this is what I want to say about the cautious designer. It will take time for him to acquire a hand. It may be attractive or it may not, but it will be his own.

The bolder young designer, on the other hand, may consider the past examples of bookcraft too tame. He will want to dress them up, or even go for "the big splash." He may be thoroughly dissatisfied with the popular type faces and with the fairly standardized type face sizes. He may not immediately realize that a book is not a poster or a package on the shelves of a supermarket. (We are discussing here, of course, only the typography and binding design, not the book jacket.) And so he may try to shock rather than please the reader, using typographic or occasionally even color devices. In this process the book makes a not-so subtle transition from, as it were, an invisible container for the written word, to a dressed-up showcase.

The young designer, who builds up the typography or binding design, or both, to demonstrate his own talent is competing rather arrogantly with the writer. Presumably he does so because he doesn't yet know any better.

Of course, these views apply to the book that consists mainly of text—fiction and other straight reading matter. Where the book involves a great deal of

pictorial material, or where a small amount of pictorial material is of great importance, other values
apply. Here, the designer will have more of an opportunity to design. He will also, probably, be made
more aware of his lack of experience. In general, he
will overcome this lack by learning from those who
have worked at book design much longer than he
has.

Let us consider three basic kinds of books: Simple,
non-controversial fiction and nonfiction; textbooks;
and what, for want of a better name, might be called
special projects—including coffee table books, gift
items, art books, and ambitious sets.

Simple fiction and nonfiction is still "dressed up,"
I am afraid, more than it is designed. Simplicity—not
to be confused with plainness—remains at a pre-
mium in fiction design. In general, the designing of
fiction and nonfiction, even with illustrations, does
not present any great problems unless, of course, the
designer finds out after having designed the entire
book that what was expected of him was quite different from what he thought. Perhaps he will be
given "a free hand"—and that contains an element
of danger, since it may open the way to criticism after
the event. The designer should pin down his employer in advance so as to find out at least whether
he is expected to design in a traditional manner or in a
more "modern," or unconventional way.

Designing textbooks requires someone who is interested in the material. It is true that many textbooks, those at the college level in particular, cannot be understood by the designer, but a feeling of interest can reduce this handicap. If the author is not available, the editors are usually most helpful and understanding.

Illustrations chosen to be used in textbooks are often of a motley nature. The sources may include new and old photographs, many of the latter richly decorated with old crop marks in crayon. Some sources may be pages torn out of old textbooks, and sometimes the designer cannot be sure which side of the page to use. Some of the less experienced artists engaged to illustrate textbooks have a way of supplying the design with art of many sizes. Then, if the larger sizes are reduced to match up with the smaller ones, the lines in the larger illustrations become much too fine, and if captions have been lettered on them, these become too small. The whole question of how to treat captions should, of course, be worked out in advance: Will all captions be typeset? Will old lettering or new lettering or both be utilized?

These and many other questions are for the textbook designer to determine. It is he who must clearly understand all the design problems in a book. Is the house designer up to it? If, in addition to basic talent, he has sufficient experience, it is best to keep the job in the house. For one thing, it makes communications more efficient. On the other hand, it can be argued that the presumably peaceful atmosphere of a private studio may enable a free-lance designer to do a better job.

A few words on special projects—heavily illustrated books—costly titles which must be impressive to be salable, as they often have little editorial content: picture books, usually dramatic in content and design (the more dramatic, the more bleeding of pictures); lavishly illustrated cookbooks (almost too beautiful to be used in the kitchen, and really intended as conversation pieces); books on interior decorating; books on flower arrangement; books printed on stocks of different colors; books with costly bindings and plenty of acetate, and books bound in strange materials.

Such books are usually not designed in the house. The designer who creates them will generally be required to work with a special editor and with the author (who is usually out of town), sometimes also with a photographer who is new at the game, and more often than not the designer rues the day he took on the assignment. How could he have anticipated how much "designing" would be done by these collaborators? How could he have known how willing they would be to take up a great deal of time, including his own, to get the book just as *they* visualized it? And if the production manager has told the designer in advance, "This is your baby!" who really is the final arbiter?

A strange attitude, all too commonly found, is that of the majority of religious publishers, which is simply that a minimum of design seems to satisfy their needs. Jackets are mostly simple, adequate jobs, no more. The argument is, of course, that the runs are small and the budget cannot stand even standard expenditures for design, plates, and presswork. What the religious publishers underestimate is the need to compete not only with other books in the store window, but on library shelves. Like all other books which have some element that makes reading an effort, such as schoolbooks, technical books—and for that matter—promotional books, every effort has to be made to make the reading of such books as pleasurable as possible. The other day I saw a book, the history of an important State of the Union, obviously printed by a legal printer. It certainly looked it!

Twenty years ago, most medical books looked horrible, as did nearly all the college texts. The changes of the last decades are absolutely amazing and often equally stunning. Clearly the result of demand for better appearance, consequently, there has risen a competition among textbook publishers. Money can be expended on this group of books more readily than on many trade books or on religious books.

When there is little money available but an earnest desire to produce attractive books, the solution is resourcefulness. Just as a mother, a scoutmaster, a teacher, and even an amateur cook can produce miracles with a little ingenuity, so the person whose task it is to produce books can replace the buckeye approach with original ideas. If I say, first of all, give yourself a little time, I don't mean a half year of leaving the manuscript on the desk. What I do mean is going after the editorial departments and getting them to come through a little faster. One of the most inexcusable excuses is, "We lost so much time, now we must get the manuscript out tomorrow." After that it will take two days to get to the printer, two more days until it gets to the composing room and a working week is shot.

In an industry that teems with deadlines and crises, one rewarding though infrequent opportunity is the chance to design an art book.

After an era of very dull art books, we have seen many which are classic or near-classic in design. Careful consideration is usually given to them, as their production cost is very high. Usually much more time is allotted to their design and production than to that of most other books. When a designer is lucky enough to be in on the production of an art book from its very inception, he is fortunate indeed.

An initial meeting with the author or editor, also with the production manager, and perhaps even with the printer, will soon enough establish the ground rules. Basic facts will be discussed and perhaps agreed upon without too much of a battle or delay. An art book consists of text and illustrations. A decision has to be made about the process by which the book is to be printed, what trim size will be suitable, and how many pages the book should have. These considerations, of course, are part of the inevitable cost-production-sales formula. Two main facts will emerge: a production schedule and a retail price.

When the manuscript and illustrative materials have been cleared by the editorial department, the designer, hoping he has the blessing of the production department, can start his work. If he can work with the author, so much the better. Together, author and designer can take care of many technical and esthetic problems. It is my experience that preparing illustrative material can take from four to five times as much time as the original design.

The designer probably will not be as familiar with a specific topic as is the author. Therefore, collaboration makes good sense. Even if the author should spend several weekends in your home or work with you day and night, everyone will fare better ultimately. The author may insist on emphasizing or de-emphasizing certain illustrative material for editorial reasons; the designer may look at the arrangement merely from an esthetic point of view.

If the first layouts and sample pages are produced to the satisfaction of the publisher, it is necessary to have a printer print layout pages showing the size and position of type columns (area), single or double, also the trim size and a ⅛ inch bleed area for two facing pages. All layouts should be visualized and produced in double spreads. It is advisable for the designer to plan for himself a series of diversified types of layouts—for example, full pages of illustration including caption—the caption might even be on the opposite page, half pages, quarter pages, and a variety of easy-to-handle layout solutions such as having one illustration on the left-hand page and three small ones on the right-hand page. The designer will find out soon enough that such a plan cannot be followed merely by letting layout B follow layout A, etc. He will also realize that even a variety of layouts will not be sufficient, but it will help him to work with basic sizes.

Naturally, the sizes of illustrations should not be rigid. On the other hand, a book in which every illustration is of a slightly different size will look fairly jumbled. Consequently, there will be a certain amount of uniformity; there will be exceptions to the rules; there will be very special, sometimes even intricate, layout problems. Illustrations may be square halftones, they may be vignetted, they may be line illustrations of irregular shapes which will in turn supply an element of change.

In fact, change of pace, a change from large to small illustrations and vice versa, can be very exciting. Perhaps some will need to bleed, perhaps some will not lend themselves to it.

In fairness to the creative work of an artist, even a photographer, cropping should be avoided where possible. There are many schools of thought on this. One of them is that since books are comparatively small, art has to be reduced substantially from its original size. Thus, the larger it appears on the page, the better.

Primary or rough layouts can be produced by two basic methods. One is to indicate by squares or shapes illustrations in their proper reduction on the layout pages, together with the text, which, of course, should have already been set. The other and more popular method is to paste stats or blueprints of the illustrations down along with galley proofs and, if possible, even printed captions.

In the basic deliberations when the length of the book has been determined, the designer must decide how much of the available space is absolutely needed for the text and the captions, so that he can tell the amount of space available for the illustrations. Naturally, he will want to establish an agreeable relationship between the illustrations and the size and design of the type. In large art books the type measure is often that of the double column, or it may be a single column set fairly wide.

As the designer proceeds with the layouts or paste-ups—and this point cannot be emphasized enough—it is most advisable to establish a certain space formula and to check it every ten pages. By that I mean that it is easy to check off the number of pages the type alone will absorb, including, of course, headings and captions, and therefore to know what percentage of space may be used for just the illustrations.

By careful checking, the designer will always know from checkpoint to checkpoint whether his design runs ahead or behind the proper percentage, and by making illustrations somewhat larger or smaller, he will be able to control the next group of pages.

It is a terrible experience to find out at the end of the job that the book is three or five pages too long, in which case many layouts must be done over to save small amounts of space. It is hard to describe to a beginner how time-consuming such an operation is. If you should run a few pages short, no great harm is done. Perhaps an illustration or two can easily be inserted towards the end, assuming that everything has to be done in double spreads. It is easy to insert or delete two facing pages, but adding or deleting a single page makes all subsequent layouts go out of kilter.

Just about the hardest layout problem to solve is changing positions of illustrations and captions.

When they say to you, "picture #41 was #52 and now is #28 and will go with caption #33 which you will probably find on page 33 or 34 but in the dummy on page 30 or 31" and when this cute little transaction takes place 100 times in a 192 page book—well, wouldn't you scream? I wish I had a dollar for every reader who will not believe me and maybe five dollars for each of those who do!

However, I stand ready to substantiate this story although I have been pledged not to reveal the names of the "innocents." And quite naturally, when this book eventually is published someone in my family or in my neighborhood is bound to say: "What pretty pictures! You must have had so much fun designing this book!" *Fun, indeed!*

I have said before that in all this it is good to have the author at your side. It will be fun too, and considerably more stimulating than working without him. I have had more pleasure out of collaborating with authors than in being entirely on my own. This is not to be construed as false modesty. Authors have design ideas, and designers can be articulate in their opinions, too.

In regard to the front matter and the basic chapter headings, I will only say that the better they are integrated, the finer your book will be. I find over-dressed title pages obtrusive, particularly in the case of art books where, after all, enough esthetic pleasure is provided in the pages of the book. It can only be hoped that all the front matter, from half title to contents page, and whatever back matter there is, such as the index, can be designed in one sitting in order to integrate it as well as possible.

A word on the binding and the book jacket. I believe that more than any other category, the art book requires a one-man job of design. Since an art book usually contains photographs or art in black and white or even color, the typographer should be able to produce a "selling" jacket as well, if not better, than an artist specializing in jackets. The reason for that is very simply that no one knows the book better from a pictorial point of view. As for the binding of art books, their sizes and often substantial weights require substantial strength. Do hold out for good cover materials and insist on the best boards available. Headbands help to keep the backbone in shape. As far as the color and the binding design are concerned, I don't want to say anything except that they should be in keeping with the book. I am remembering with a certain amount of discomfort an art book I designed with good typography, a good jacket, and a very indifferent binding. I thought then that restraint was important, but I fear I restrained myself too much.

A last word, on end papers. Art books are full of illustrations in color. Further illustrations or maps on end papers, unless absolutely necessary, are gilding the lily. There are available, at low cost, many fine end paper sheets in unusual textures and colors. It is advisable to utilize a decided contrast with the text paper for this last touch.

Recently, I was involved in the design and production of a book for an author who had not quite decided whether to publish his book himself or to offer it to a publisher. Eventually, he did succeed in making an arrangement with a publisher. The book has had two substantial printings, but my story deals with its jacket. The particular jacket in question was commissioned by the publisher, not by the author. With not too much effort, a package came into being that involved four people, namely, the author, the publisher, the jacket artist, and myself. Bookcover materials, colors, and type faces were compared and matched in a spirit of cooperation.

This, however, is not always the case. Sometimes, someone in such a combine is opinionated and headstrong. On other occasions it is simply a matter of now knowing what the book is about or interpreting it incorrectly. Such was the case when I innocently prepared a very conservative, very delicate, binding design for a book titled *Sleep in Peace.* "Something about the Victorian Age," I was told, as I remember. I never saw the manuscript. When the book was printed, bound, and jacketed, I was shocked. The jacket design by Artzybasheff was dramatic, sharp in colors, and depicted a scene of labor unrest in

Britain. Since then, I make it my business to inquire more carefully.

The trouble is that, in all large and in many medium-size houses, the job of supervising book design and the job of supervising jacket design are usually handled by two different people. Being pressured and beset by standard crises, they do not always get together on every book, and, of course, there are always the sales and advertising departments to contend with. One answer to this problem is more experienced personnel. Another way to improve the situation is to work out schedules in a more realistic manner, perhaps by making the editors "come through" on time. Naturally, the momentum of a production schedule builds up. Gentle at first (the editors might waste very precious days, even weeks, allowing the manuscripts to linger on their desks), the pace quickens, and later on, copy editors and indexers can use up a great deal of time too. Getting cost estimates often consumes far too much time, particularly when several estimates are wanted. By the time the book is on press, it is often so close to the publication date that the binder is asked to make up for lost time. There usually is not much time given to typographic and jacket design as well as production. It is quite understandable how signals can get crossed—but hardly excusable.

A typographer must come to grips with many problems at one time or another. They usually fall into three groups, namely esthetic, production, and cost problems. Quite obviously, there is a wide range, and the varieties are colorful and rarely dull. As in the weaving of a rug or in the making of a mosaic, eventually a pattern or design evolves in which personalities, talents, techniques, and finances are mixed.

For some reason that I cannot immediately analyze, I have always been particularly interested in series of books. Even as a youngster I was attracted by certain large advertisements offering for sale literally hundreds of titles, books in just about any field. I am sure I was "sold" by the stimulating titles such as *A Thousand Tricks, How to Perform Them*, or *How to Build a Miniature Steam Engine*, etc. These little German books, probably first cousins to the well-known blue books in this country, sold then for only a few pennies. I know I purchased many of them. Whether or not I read all of them with the same interest, I do not remember.

Through the years I have continued my interest in sets of books—encyclopedias, collected works. I have designed them, and I believe that I have found myself drawn to them because of the fact that after designing a prototype for a series, designing the rest became considerably easier. To be sure, in textbook series, new typographical problems were abundant. In how-to-do-it or in art books, layouts were similar in their *general* planning but there were new, *specific* layout problems on every page.

A true designer has to be also something of an editor, certainly a knowledgeable production man, and must have in mind publicity and sales considerations, too. He is not expected to be a jack-of-all-trades, but some knowledge in areas related to his work is necessary to produce a successful design.

As I sort the mail, weeding out the unwanted advertising from congressmen and supermarkets, I am happy to recognize the familiar handwriting of son Peter on an envelope stamped New Haven, Connecticut, or else that of daughter Steffie from Storrs, Connecticut. Were her communication to show a cancellation from Princeton, New Jersey, or his letter to come from Poughkeepsie, New York, I would probably be more than a little puzzled.

In much the same manner, the characteristic book design by W. A. Dwiggins in a book published by New Directions or the Museum of Modern Art would have surprised me some twenty-five years ago.

W. A. Dwiggins and Alfred A. Knopf were almost synonymous. I know that Dwiggins did a little work for Little, Brown and Co. and of course, created some of the best type faces for the Linotype Company, but as far as book design was concerned, his work belonged to Knopf. In fact, Mr. Knopf more than anyone else in this country established book design not only as something desirable, but also as a "house style."

When a designer's work has as distinctive and recognizable a face as some people's handwriting, it may supersede the requirements of very different types of books. While some of the very typical Dwiggins ornaments on bindings, including his special sense of color combinations, may have been used a little too uniformly on books of varying character, he certainly created the right format for each book.

His excellent typographical taste and knowledge made it possible for him to mix type faces in a manner which might have caused many other designers considerable grief. He could also add his own calligraphy which, like his own typographical ornaments, fitted in with the text and front matter.

In short, he was a master, and Mr. Knopf very wisely recognized that.

At present, there is much more book design than there was twenty or thirty years ago. The book design departments of many of the large publishing houses have work for quite a few designers, including free lances. A true house style is hardly possible any more. On the other hand, there are some book manufacturers who maintain small design departments for the benefit of a great number of their customers. Whether, in such a case, the manufacturer's designer should in effect establish a house style for the plant is debatable. A good designer's work is distinctive, yet as house style it may be applied to a number of publishers whose books and general character differ.

In my own experience with a manufacturer, supplying book designs for many publishers, I attempted to maintain as much of the house style of different publishers as possible. Frankly, I wonder if I was very successful in that endeavor; I know that my *own* style could still be recognized. There are, of course, technical limitations in each plant. Some type faces are available and favored, and this alone can create a certain impression. My wish in those years to design properly and maintain my integrity created some conflicts. I have had to make some compromises, I hope not too many, but, I am sure, more than did Mr. Dwiggins.

The other day I was shown a small portfolio of ephemera—the little odd jobs a printer does, such as stationery, tickets, announcements. They are nothing startling, but they had a few things in common. First of all, they were all exceedingly well printed. The colors the printer used were in sophisticated taste. The type was well selected, the type ornaments were of the variety popular through two or three centuries but ending with Bodoni and finally the Bauhaus. Surely, all in all, a most conservative man behind it all. And who was holding the composing stick, the gauge? Who was carefully, patiently setting the type, the ornaments? One of the nation's foremost graphic artists, modern, way-out, anything at all but conservative. What a double life he must lead! I'd hate to sleep through *his* nightmares, with grim horrifying art fighting off cases of florets, of pastel-colored printing inks and lovely mould-made papers.

Book design is a very complex job with many facets, and two of the most useful qualities of the book designer are a good memory and an ability to handle figures rapidly.

Some years back I found myself in the New York office of an out-of-town book manufacturer. While we were exchanging pleasantries, he pointed to a manuscript and told me that I was to design it. I looked at it for a moment or two, weighing it in my hands reflectively, and I said, "5⅜ by 8, 11 on 13 Granjon, 23 by 36, 352 pages, $3.95." The manufacturer looked at me for a moment. Then he turned over the manuscript to a secretary and asked her to cast it off, telling her casually that the type would be 11 on 13 Granjon, 23 by 36 picas. The young lady went into her own office where she presumably proceeded to measure the width of average typewritten lines, adding also depth of all pages, and, in fact, going through all the motions of working out the exact length of the manuscript. She never came back while I was still visiting, but the manufacturer called me the next day saying, "The girl came back to my office at the end of the afternoon. She figured the book would make 352 pages. How did you do it?" I told him that this was my trade secret, but I am willing to tell it to you.

By thumbing through it very rapidly, I could see that it was a clean manuscript running from page one to 410. I could see that the typewriter used was pearl, which indicated to me that there would be 12 characters to an inch. The average page I knew would be about 6 inches wide, and this gave me 72 characters. The average page would also be between 8 and 9 inches deep, and this averaged 25 lines. I knew 72 x 25 was 1,800; 1,800 multiplied by 370 I figured to be roughly 640,000 characters. The book was a novel with an average number of chapters— 14 or 15—and I figured that 23 picas (average measure for the standard 5⅜ by 8 size of fiction) would yield about 60 characters per line. Thirty-six pica in depth would give me 33 lines of 13 pt. type, so 60 x 33 was roughly 2,000. Dividing the length of the manuscript, 640,000, by 2,000 gave me 320 pages. Allowing about 20 odd pages for chapter breaks and front matter brought me close to 352 pages, which is the nearest multiple of 32 pages. A sheet usually contains 64 pages on each side. To call a sales price was merely a little extra knowledge of what novels sold for at that moment. It really was easy, but of course this is not the way to design a book, and not every manuscript is clean.

The teacher is an old hand at designing books, knows book production, equipment, and people.

The student, a talented artist, has no experience with book design, but is willing to tackle the job.

Teacher: The package in this mail looks like a manuscript. Would you like to examine it?

Student: It's a lot of yellow paper, it looks very messy. There are illustrations, some are black on white, some are white on black.

T: Those are negative and positive photostats. See if you can match them. Are there any numbers on them?

S: Yes, but they are very mixed up.

T: Put them in order numerically. First the black on white, the positive ones. Then the negative ones. See if there are any numbers missing.

Any mention of the time elapsed in the performing of every task described here is tactfully omitted.

S: There are some numbers missing, and there are some duplications.

T: The duplications may either be errors or be slightly different things that *look* like duplications. You must be very careful to see whether they are not slightly different.

S: You're right. Here's one which is an outline drawing. The other one has some shading in the same outline.

T: Now put the illustrations aside in two separate

piles and let's get an accurate castoff of the manu-script.

S: Is this a manuscript? What is a castoff?

T: Written matter that is to become a book is a manuscript. Even if it's typed and even if it's messy. The castoff is the calculation which will tell you how long the manuscript is. You have to measure the width and the depth of the pages.

S: All the pages?

T: Yes. But be sure to notice whether this manu-script is numbered consecutively. Also there may be some pages which are only a few lines long.

S: After page 18 there follows a number of pages marked 18 A, 18 B, 18 C, etc. There is no page 63, and page 82 has only 8 lines and a long pencil line from the bottom of the text to the bottom of the page.

T: Add all the pages no matter how they are num-bered. Some pages may be short. If so, count them as half or quarter pages. Now hold your ruler under an average line of text and see how long the line is.

S: This line is 5¾ inches wide, but some are wider and some are shorter, so this would be average, wouldn't it? Now what do I do?

T: We are setting out to find the length of the manuscript in characters. If you feel that 5¾ inches is an average line, but you must check at least 10 or 12 pages, you still don't know how many characters are on each line. Count how many characters make one inch. It will probably be 12 or 10. You want to be very careful to see if different parts of the manuscript have been typed on different typewriters.

S: Now that I have measured a number of pages, I find that the line is really 6 inches on an average, and there are 12 characters on each inch. Now what?

T: Now you must determine how deep the average page is. If it is double-spaced, as are most manuscripts, it will probably vary from 26 to 28 lines per page. Three double-spaced lines make an inch. Hold the inch ruler vertically across the page. What do you find?

S: It is about 8¾ inches deep.

T: An easier way is to say, 8 inches plus 2 lines, or if you like, 9 inches minus one line. The pages will probably average close to 9 inches.

S: I counted 112 pages in all and the text makes 874 inches, but there are several pages in the beginning which are really not text pages.

T: This is the front matter. There probably is a half-title, a title page, a copyright page and a contents page, maybe more. Do you know what a half-title is?

S: No.

T: The half-title is usually the first page in a book. It carries the title of the book and nothing else. It can be followed by a blank page, or a frontispiece, which is sometimes an illustration or sometimes carries a list of books by the same author. Occasionally, it is combined with a title page for a so-called double spread title page. On the back of the title page we have the copyright page which carries copyright and Library of Congress information. Sometimes the name of the printer and that of the designer appear on this page too.

S: Then I really have only 104 pages of text and some of those pages where the chapters begin, have only half as much text.

T: Since we are using the space above the text for the chapter titles, we will consider them full pages. I hope you realize, by the way, that we must count the spaces between the words as characters. Now multiply the number of characters per average line with the number of lines per average page and multiply that by the number of pages.

S: That would be 72 x 25 x 104?

T: Quite correct. That makes 187,200 characters —right?

With the help of paper and pencil and some coffee, the student obtains the same result. Both teacher and student are satisfied. On to the next hurdle.

S: Where do we go from here? Would it be a big book? How will I know what type to use?

T: First of all, read the letter which probably is in the same package with the manuscript and the photostats. It should give you important data: if the publisher, or rather the production manager, requested anything specific or they are leaving it to us. Try to find out who will set and print this book and how many copies are going to be made and at what price the book should be sold. See if there is any mention made of the kind of paper to be used. Read the letter carefully, it may contain important information.

S: (Reads) "Dear Designer: We are sending you by same mail manuscript and illustrations for the new book of our favorite author: *How to Write a How To Do It Yourself Book.* We would like the book to be 8½x11 inches, about 160 pages long. It will be printed in black and white, including 62 illustrations, 30 of them line, the rest halftones. We are not quite sure who will set the job. Please use some type which is easily available. Some of the front matter is still to come. The book will be printed by offset, and we will use a nice 60 pound sheet. For the binding, please use a three-piece cover with a B-grade backbone and colored paper sides. Perhaps you will want to use the same stock for ends. Use one-hit foil in two or three colors.

The author is presently away in Bermuda so please do not ask for any changes or request additional illustrations.

May we have your specifications and sketches for sample pages *very soon.* With best regards, etc., etc."

T: Is there anything that you don't understand?

S: There is very little I *do* understand.

The designer decides to put the manuscript aside and to explain to his assistant the strange lingo of the production department. As this step is practically a monologue and very time-consuming, the reader can be spared the agonies of listening. Eventually, work is resumed.

T: We must now begin to design the text. The publisher has requested the use of a type face which is readily available. You have read many books. Do you have a favorite type face?

S: I really don't know what a type face is, or what their names are. I just know that I liked some books better than others, that they seemed to be easier to read.

T: Take a type book from our shelf, one that says machine faces. Go through it and see if there are some type faces you recognize or like, even if you don't know them. Take your time about it, and don't try to compare them to each other. Just pick one that you like.

S: There are many attractive type faces in this book. Does it matter what size I select?

T: It matters a great deal. Remember, we are working with a little less than 190,000 characters and we also have 66 illustrations to work with. Now tell me how big the illustrations are. Would they make full pages, or half-pages, or what?

S: There are 15 illustrations which look like full pages to me and there are 41 which would take half-pages, I guess, unless you could get more than 2 on a page. The rest are very small.

T: Of course, the illustrations may also have captions, although they were not mentioned in the letter.

S: Oh, I see them now—some typewritten lines pasted on the bottom of the illustrations.

T: If you have 15 full pages and about 40 half pages, that would give us another 20 full pages; so all told, we have about 35-36 pages of illustrations. There were a few pages of front matter, probably 8, that adds up to 44 pages. The publisher wants 160 pages. Forty-four from 160 leaves 116 pages. Divide the 190,000 characters by 116 and you get about 1630 characters per page. Now you must find a type which will give us approximately 1630 characters per page. Remember the page size is rather large, $8\frac{1}{2}$x11 inches, because it is an illustrated book.

Cut a piece of paper $8\frac{1}{2}$x11 inches. Now draw a rectangle on this page to represent the type page. The type page is the area occupied by the type. The illustrations may be smaller, the same size, or even larger than the type page, but the type should stay within a standard measure.

This is a big book and we will use large margins. Make yourself a one inch mark from the left edge, $1\frac{1}{4}$ inch from the top, $1\frac{1}{2}$ inch from the right, and $2\frac{1}{4}$ inches from the bottom. Now draw the box. It will be 6 inches wide and $7\frac{1}{2}$ inches in height. Perhaps we shall extend it in depth, but we shall see.

S: It looks very nice now. What type can we use on this.

T: It is a large page, so the type must be large too, but we must fit into this box. Try for something in 12 point.

S: I like Caledonia and Garamond. They seem different, but both are easy to read.

T: We may try Caledonia, but you must work out the amount of space between the lines, the "leading."

S: It says here, 12 point Caledonia, 3 point leaded. Is that what you mean?

T: Yes. Perhaps 12 point Caledonia will work out all right. You remember that the width of the type page is six inches and, since an inch equals six picas, we are working with 36 picas. As far as I remember, 12 point Caledonia sets 2¼ characters per pica, which means that we will have about 80 characters per line. This is about 10 percent longer than lines we are used to reading, but the type face you have selected has a good deal of color and is easy to read. I would think that I would want to use even one point more leading on such a big page. Tell me how many lines there will be on this page?

S: Well, I know that the type page is 7½ inches deep and I guess I have to multiply that by six and that makes 45 picas. Would that be 45 lines?

T: No. You forgot the leading. You figured out correctly that the page is 45 picas deep, but in order to know the number of lines you must multiply the picas by 12, as each pica has 12 points, and then divide the result by 16; 12 point type plus 4 point leading makes 16. Now remember, 45 picas multiplied by 12 points equals 540 points. Divide that by 16 and you get 34 lines. Actually 34 lines times 16 would equal 544 points, but we don't worry about those extra 4 points, especially since the leading under the last line doesn't show anyway and the descenders are probably not too many.

S: What are descenders?

T: The upward strokes of a, b, d, k, and l are called ascenders, so the downward strokes of a g, p, y or q are called descenders, but you will note that there are never very many on any given line. We have not figured out yet how many characters per page we have. Remember I said the line would be about 80 characters long. If we multiply that by 34, we get over 2700 characters per page. Now you remember that all we needed per page was 1630 characters and our count shows us that we can conveniently accommodate a thousand more characters per page. We are, therefore, faced with a variety of possibilities. (1) the book might be shorter—perhaps 128 pages. This decision is not up to us, however. (2) We can give the illustrations a great deal more play, perhaps put some of the smaller illustrations on a page by themselves. This would be alright if the book is primarily a picture book.

S: Isn't it? There are so many illustrations.

T: Yes, but from what you tell me they illustrate the text, but they don't seem to be the main thing such as reproductions of paintings in an art book. There is another solution. We can set the type quite differently, perhaps smaller, but also much shorter and vary the number of lines per page, so that we will use the type very much like blocks of illustrations. Since you said that the illustrations are not square but irregular, the square blocks of type will offer a pleasant contrast. They will be in the true sense *mise en page* which is French for layout and means literally "put on the page."

S: How will I go about finding the right type and the right size?

T: First, go back to the type books and study them a little. There are many attractive type faces available. Why don't you pick some picture books out of my library and look them over. This will give you ideas and you may even understand what may have motivated the designer to use the type faces he did. I think I should warn you at this point not to try too hard to use type faces which are "suitable" to the text. Remember, the prime consideration of designing a book is to make reading a pleasure and not to provide a showcase for art of the designer. You will find that you can and, in fact, will probably have to use the same type face for very different types of books.

S: How many type faces are there?

T: I have never counted them, but there are hundreds and yet the book industry somehow favors only a few dozen designs. Of course, they come in different sizes and are sometimes mixed in such a way that they can look very different from another book done in the same type face. There's also a very substantial amount of interesting contrast available to the designer by using the large sizes, in conjunction with the "text type."

I realize that book design may seem very complex to you and that you will have to learn a great deal. You must, in fact, be willing to become a book architect, so to speak, and at the same time become adept as a juggler of the black and the white which is after all the essence of any printed matter. Most of all, you must love books.

Some summers ago, after a visit at the shore of Maine, I found my way inland where I could enjoy a music festival and at the same time do some work —which inevitably I had taken along, and which, inevitably, I did not do until after my return home. I thought about it, but pencils and pica rulers stayed away from paper.

The job in hand was the simultaneous design of two books, using the same manuscript, one being a large paperback with a small number of pages, and the other, a smaller, hardcover book with at least twice as many pages. In the first instance it was a question of designing in such a way as to make the reader feel that the text was attractive and legible, the illustrations sizable and plentiful. In the second case, the goal was to prevent the reader from feeling that the book had been padded—that is, the text set larger than necessary and more white space used than needed. Still, for both, the material was the same.

It is in the nature of publishing to utilize "properties" more than once. This is particularly true with illustrated books. Any publisher will tell you that one of his most difficult tasks is to find the proper market for any given book, or to create the right book for an established market. For some years, it has been a very understandable practice to create such books with different formats and different prices (but the same title) simultaneously.

I have always thought of such books as a challenge for the designer. In a way, such a two-pronged problem is amusing and very paradoxical, a bit like something from *Alice in Wonderland*.

The manuscript in this particular case contained 50 pages, averaging 27 lines with roughly 65 characters each. Thus each page averaged 1,755 characters, the length of the book was 88,000 characters.

In the paperback, there being 44 pages (out of 48) at my disposal for text and illustrations, and 40 illustrations requiring 22 pages, the remaining 22 pages given to text had only to accommodate 88,000 characters divided by 22, or 4,000 characters per page.

The trim size 10¼ x 7½ inches, made a double column feasible, the oblong trim size 24 picas wide and 36 picas in depth. Thus, if we had 72 picas depth per page and set the text on a 13 point slug, perhaps in a 10 point or 11 point face, we would divide 14,000 characters by 66 lines and the result—60—would indicate the number of characters per line. As we planned to set each line 24 picas wide we therefore looked for a suitable type face in 10 or 11 point which would set 64 characters on a 24 pica line, or 2.5 characters per pica. There are a large number of such type faces.

Consider, however, that the manuscript might easily have been 10 pages longer or that we might have felt the illustrations should have more prominence. If the length of the manuscript had been 100,000 characters, allowing only 20 pages for the text, the situation would have been quite different. We would then have had to accommodate 5,000 characters per page. That would have meant extending the measure (or length) of each line to 25 picas, the depth of the page to 38 picas, and would have given us 76 lines if we had stayed with a 12 point slug, setting type either 10/12 or 11/12. If the latter were ruled out to avoid creating a page set too tightly, we then would have had to find 10 point type faces which set 2.6 characters per pica. We could then proceed with the design, always being careful not to use too much space. If, on the other hand, everything works out as planned, it is most gratifying to see the length of a short book come out right on the nose.

A note of caution: It is imperative always to check every few pages to see that the number of pages allotted to text and illustrations is not exceeded. Repairing damage can make a job take several times longer than it would if carefully and constantly checked. A long book is, naturally, easier to adjust than a short one.

It is not unusual to publish a title in different formats at different prices for different markets. In this particular case, the first task was to fit a rather short manuscript, plus a fair number of illustrations, into 48 pages, as I have described. The second task was to create an even more attractive book in hardcovers of an entirely different size. The number of pages was doubled; single columns replaced the double column format of the paperbound edition.

The new format decided upon was $7\frac{1}{4} \times 8\frac{1}{2}$ inches. This was an agreeable size, almost a square shape like that of the books introduced into this country by Albert Skira. The problem was to give the reader a pleasant book with generous margins without creating a feeling that the book had been padded. In addition, a physical limitation both of time and money was imposed by the publisher's request not to have the new type reset for the hardcover edition.

There are many ways to do a good job. It is a matter of taste, skill, and naturally, experience. In this particular case, a very generous margin was supplied at the top and at the left of each page (left pages as well as right pages). In the other edition, four illustrations had filled a page, here, two looked even better. A substantial amount of space was allotted to captions to emphasize them. The page numbers were set well into the margin.

This book was printed by offset. Had it been printed by letterpress, there would have been other considerations to deal with. The proof of the pudding is that no one at the publishing house seems to know any more which edition came first, the paperback or the hardcover. I do, but I will not tell.

The hardcover edition, of course, necessitated a jacket, and that, done in a very different style from that of the paper cover, emphasized the substantial difference between the two editions.

In another case of varying format, a cookbook had been compiled and sold to one of the paperback publishers. At that time, however, paperbacks were assumed to be reprints; therefore, when the book was in pages, reproduction proofs were pulled and the type then packaged neatly to be used some eighteen months later. In the meantime, the type was blown up 15 percent, again photomechanically, the text printed in black with the headings in two additional colors (one to each side of the sheet). In fact, because this did not represent any technical difficulties, these headings were uniformly pulled two or three picas into the left margin. Thus the stage was set to print a three-color, $5 or $6 cookbook, 6 x 9, on good stock and in an attractive binding. All of this was from the modest 20 x 30 pica measure of the black and white type page that was later printed on wood pulp paper. I must say that I have always enjoyed such metamorphoses of type matter. While I am aware and glad of the traditional aspects of the book as opposed to the package, I occasionally like to have a hand in playing variations on the same theme.

That it is in the nature of the human beast never to be satisfied with what is available, is not a new story. "Imported from France" lends prestige to a silk scarf. Italy is the magic word for things made of leather, Switzerland supplies us with the finest watches. But not always. Many a watch hearing the proud "Made in Switzerland" label is just as inferior a mass article as if it had been manufactured in Japan or in Jersey City. Likewise, "Made in America" may look good on some articles but not on all. It is particularly amusing that the best delicatessen stores on both sides of the Atlantic feature, as costly specialties, canned goods imported from "the other side."

Two years ago I designed a book in which about one hundred photographs were at least as important as the text. The production problem was obvious: Get it done well and cheaply. Done well meant sheet

fed gravure, preferably with the text done by letterpress; done cheaply meant do it all by offset.

A happy enough compromise arose out of a cha-
otic situation. We used the best sheet fed gravure,
but gave up the idea of the text done by letterpress.
And in order to be able to afford the best gravure
printer, the photographer was willing to give up his
part of the royalties. His offer was accepted.

Now for the "man bites dog" twist. Subsequently
the rights to the book were sold to a reputable German publisher. He had the translation printed in
Switzerland using our layouts and negatives throughout. He did select an offset printer in Switzerland and
the result was disastrous. The presswork was horrible.

It is certainly not unusual to be asked to produce
something unusual—a book jacket or a binding design. Naturally there is not to be any unusual cost
as part of this operation. I daresay it would have
been too usual in the particular case I am referring
to, simply to select and purchase an unusual cover
stock and order it.

So I took a few pieces of handy end paper stock
and requested the foreman of the airbrush department (by the name of Brush, so help me!) to spray
parallels diagonally in bluish purple and purplish red
on the few sheets of the stock. While the paint was
still wet—sticky to the touch—I wiped across the
color sprays with a crumpled ball of newspaper, and
then in still another direction applied a small pocket

comb which I was willing to sacrifice to the cause of Art.

Everybody loved the sample cover and the book bound in this manner. Little did I foresee what was to come! Quite naturally it was nobody's real concern *how* I would produce the sheets needed to bind 3,000 books. There was no question about this having to be a hand job, as a full color reproduction would have cost far too much then (and now) for this purpose.

Before I knew it I had permission to neglect my regular book design and other typographic chores long enough to devote myself to the job of producing enough stock (with Mr. Brush) for the first edition. Clearly I had oversold myself.

I still oversell myself occasionally, but increasingly less, I am glad to say. I am making an effort to undersell myself. Naturally I am not often taken up on that. It would seem that just as one should not take a responsibility too lightly, it is dangerous to offer too much extra work which often cannot be appreciated.

One of the more gratifying experiences in the life of a book designer is the opportunity to design the binding for a pulpit Bible for a church. While most of them are available in solid if not inspired leather bindings, they can usually be obtained in folded and gathered sheets to be handsewn on tapes and bound

—not cased in—by a hand binder. Granted, there are but few of this craft left but certainly enough for this purpose. They provide fine leather bindings for private collectors and for rare book divisions of our universities. I think every designer who has ever struggled with the cheapest book cover materials and counted the square inches of imitation gold of the stamping will find it immensely rewarding to be faced with no material limitations if only once in a lifetime. He will also cherish the experience of working closely with a practitioner of a dying craft. Is it practical, is there money in it? I am afraid not.

Corriger la fortune is a French proverb which means "to correct your luck" or perhaps even "to cheat." In book design and production there is a lot of correcting of one's luck.

There is, for instance, the case of the blown-up golf book. It started out by being a modest history of American golf, which was written by a sports journalist and meant for sale in sporting goods stores.

It was intended to be a slender volume of, perhaps, 160 pages and was thus to be set economically in Old Style No. 7. When the galleys showed up on my desk I found that the entire book had been set in Old Style No. 1. What a difference! Old Style No. 7 was acceptable as an uninteresting but economical typeface. Old Style No. 1 was not economical, not acceptable, and downright ugly.

Calling the printer brought no results. "The '7' must have looked like a '1' to the people in the composing room," said the service department. "Isn't it just as good?"

We in the publisher's office sat down for a conference.

"Can't the book be reset?" asked the publisher.

"Who will pay for it?" inquired the production manager.

There was silence. The suggestion I made then was listened to with attention, surprise, and a little dismay but it was finally accepted.

As the book was planned for the fall list, I felt that instead of being in a sporting goods store only it could be sold in any place where books were sold. Since this could be the Christmas season I suggested that we convert it into a gift item. We would make a beautiful swan out of an ugly duckling.

Changing the trim size from the standard 5⅜ x 8 to almost double the size, we blew up the type, added historical photographs and printed the entire book by offset in a dark green. This softened the look of the type and gave the photographs, all summer scenes, a warm appearance. Of course, this meant, too, that the author had to obtain the photographs we needed and many were so old and bleached out that I feared they might not look like anything. But the Murray Printing Company did a great job and the reproductions looked better than the originals.

The book was bound in green buckram and stamped in—you guessed it—green and gold. It was put in a strong green slipcase and it sold very well at a considerably higher price than originally planned.

It is probably not one of the best books I have designed, but it came through strong and attractive.

Another example:

I was involved once with a book on the history of a spice company. We had been looking for an unusual stock, but at a reasonable price. Such a stock was hard to find, so we decided if we could not afford an expensive sheet, why not use a cheap one; so the book was printed on brown craft paper. We also decided to spray oil of cloves into the book and my copy has exuded this fragrance for many years.

Using unusual papers for regular books—a European specialty—is not simple. The trouble with it is that you can't always lay your hands on more of the same paper when you reprint the book. This rules out tinted papers, which can lend a great deal of interest to a book. The reason is simply that the "making order" for any special paper is fairly high, and reprinting a quantity of 5000 or 6000 copies can be undertaken only if the publisher has had the foresight to keep enough paper on hand. If, on the other hand, no such reprint is forthcoming, the publisher is stuck with paper for which he has no use.

Composition is a very different matter. Printers differ in the variety of type faces they have to offer.

Some small printers may have very fine typographical materials that the larger manufacturers do not possess. Type faces are somewhat subject to fashion, and what was "out" yesterday may be "in" again tomorrow. A neophyte in the 1960's may be attracted to type faces which designers of the 1930's and 1940's avoided.

Limitation in available type faces may dictate desirable choices. A lack of typographic variety can tighten a design perceptibly. Editors and designers may cut down on subheads and special material if they are forced to be resourceful.

I recall setting a cookbook years ago with headings of Copperplate Gothic. This type face, with its very delicate serifs, comes only in caps, and I had never used it before for any book, but it worked out very well indeed.

In the same cookbook I found myself with 12 blank pages. Rather than "cancel" or throw out eight pages which, in fact, costs money to do, I set a short heading, "Notes," and suggested to the publisher that women using cookbooks might like to add their own recipes.

In the case of another cookbook where the headings were planned in a second color and designed to be set into the margin, I obtained reproduction proofs of the pages set in regular style. Actually the headings were set within the type pages, but the printer merely needed an extra set of negatives to move the display headings into the margin. This saved a great deal of money; the "built up" type page would have cost more to set.

When it comes to the cost of presswork, proper preparation of copy is one of the money savers. Working out the length of the book so it can be printed in multiples of 32 or 64 pages is another. Yet there are times when changing from one press to another forces changes in trim size and, perhaps, more attractive and less expensive books.

Binding, the costliest part of the book, has evoked a great deal of ingenuity among designers, publishers, and binders.

The deluxe edition of Ludwig Bemelmans' *Hotel Splendide*, for example, needed something special. The atmosphere of the old Waldorf Astoria suggested brocade. Accordingly, flowery rust and green were chosen as binding colors; they were atrocious— and just right.

I have heard of a designer who wasn't satisfied with *any* book cloth available and proceeded to bind the book in plywood. To keep the paper and the "binding" together he used a bolt and a nut. This must have been a very unusual binding.

Even as a child I was very much interested in full color illustrations, which at that time were almost invariably done by lithography. There is something about the stippled method of color lithography in its many shades that I have never found in any other reproduction method. I believe that this appealed to the romantic sense of a youngster reading all kinds of books.

Later, in the 1920's, I saw the enormous lithographic stones used in a print shop producing Christmas cards. Still later, in 1950, I watched one of the workers in a lithographic plant in Switzerland. On a very small table he had propped up the artwork, which was a bouquet of flowers. On the table he had a small stone and an arrangement of brushes, tools, and acids. More of the same were next to him on another table. He was working on eight colors, of which two were different greens, one was gray, one pink, others black, red, yellow, and blue. It was his job to correct the stones without the help of cameras or screens. By looking intently at a color proof and the original art, he knew how much he needed to etch away from any of the eight stones, or where to add or emphasize. I asked him how long it had taken him to develop such a sure eye for color combinations. He said about twenty years.

It is easy to see that in our day and age we have to take more and more refuge in optical machinery, I have no idea how many bona fide lithographic plants still exist and prosper. Of course, the slow process of printing from stone has long been supplanted by offset printing, and the image from the stone can readily be transferred to a thin zinc plate.

After I turned to book design, I became actively involved with illustrations, although not with lithography. In my capacity as a designer I became acquainted with Hilda Simon, who was illustrating a number of books which I was designing. We worked together a great deal and appreciated each other's talents.

Designing her book of American butterflies was a great pleasure for me. Naturally, I was concerned with the end result; I wanted a harmonious blending of type and illustrations, some of which were black and white but, as I recall it, most in full color.

I expressed a certain amount of concern in regard to the cost of this book. A designer who is not concerned with production costs is like an architect who would import marble from Carrara for a two-family budget house, or like a housewife who does not take advantage of food and clothing sales.

"I wonder," I said, underestimating Hilda Simon, "how much the separations will come to." The layouts I was working on were put together, using galley proofs and sketches done in full color. I had not seen any finished artwork so far. Miss Simon did not answer immediately, and we proceeded to finish the dummy. We spent a little time taking tea, and after the cups were removed, I looked up expectantly. She put a large sheet of white paper on the table, and placed on that several pieces of a kind of translucent acetate. I could not fail to notice that she handled them very gingerly, taking care not to place her fingers on them, but holding them at the edges much in the same manner in which a linotype operator holds a very hot slug which has been cast seconds before.

Miss Simon explained that the material—called Dinobase (3M Company)—was extremely sensitive, that even the slightest amount of oily substance could spoil the artwork. She continued to explain that each drawing, like that of the butterfly on a twig near a flower, represented one of the four-color plates in this order: Black for the key drawing, and to deepen and accentuate dark areas, red, blue, and yellow.

She made it clear to me that these preseparated drawings would yield a negative contact print, from which the plate would then be produced in a conventional manner. After obtaining proofs of the four plates printed in proper order, she would compare the proofs with the original artwork, and could herself make the necessary corrections on the separations.

Normally, full color artwork is photographed through a series of color filters and screens. After obtaining color proofs, the corrections must be made on the negatives, or occasionally on the plate itself. It is obvious that this is a very costly procedure. It is, in fact, the very reason why the reproduction of color illustrations is billed to the publisher at several hundred dollars each. If such figures are multiplied by even a moderate number of illustrations, the production of the book can be undertaken only if a substantial run is planned—and sold.

Miss Simon explained that in the time which it took to note the necessary corrections on the progressive proofs, or merely write similar notes on the press proof, she could make the corrections herself. Inasmuch as the work of correcting would not be left to someone other than the artist, she would naturally make supreme efforts to take care of all possible improvements promptly.

Thus the artist would be satisfied, the production department, too, and the cost of correction would probably disappear entirely, as a fee for each illustration can be arranged in advance. Naturally, the artist would be expected to produce both the illustrations and the proper separations.

Even an inexperienced production person will see the advantage of buying color artwork including separations. I have not known of many artists who do this for what they are paid. However, it is in the mutual interest of publishers and artists to work out equitable arrangements, and we shall probably see more books with good color illustrations and more young artists being encouraged to do such work.

I would be unnecessarily modest if I disclaimed knowledge of colors and color mixing altogether, but I do know that it is not as easy as it seems to be. I have had to learn through the years that it is one thing to work casually with pastels, crayons, or water colors, but it is another to reproduce this work with four printing inks. I have found that frequently a seemingly simple color—for example, sanguine in various shades from dark to light—could not be reproduced with one color. I have learned that there are greens and greens, and most certainly, reds and reds.

Working with Hilda Simon on the butterfly book, I learned a new lesson. Miss Simon explained patiently how much intensity would be required on a plate like the yellow to produce the proper green by adding a shade of blue. It had been mentioned in the beginning that black would supply the key or outline, perhaps done very delicately, but would also add depth or dimension to color even where the original did not seem to contain any black. Red, too, was added to the green of a leaf, giving it a little extra life.

We know that all primary colors are contained in anything we see. What we do not know is how the eye compensates what it actually sees or senses. We know exactly how a photographic camera sees color, but it takes the human eye of an artist to compensate for the failings of the machine. I am glad of that. I can image only too well that soon color correcting devices will be invented and perfected, and that, step by step, the human element will be banned so that the machine can take over. Not being a machine myself, I view these developments with some uneasiness.

There are production methods using tinted acetates in all four process colors. They come in tones ranging from 10 percent to 100 percent. They are uniform and are easily recognizable by an experienced eye. Miss Simon does not have to use standard process colors. Naturally, she plans her artwork that way. However, I feel that the colors are fresh and realistic, and that she could probably handle any color combination. The miraculous thing remains this: How can she know how much red is in a green leaf, how much in a seemingly yellow butterfly?

I have mentioned before that the negatives are contacts, and that there is no screen or screen formation involved. It is this feature which keeps her usually delicate drawings so true to life, for no matter how small the screen, it is hard to get used to squares in round things. It is obvious that there must be a substitute for the screen, that the acetate cannot be perfectly smooth. Actually, the old Dinobase, and a more readily available product now coming from Europe, both have an irregularly grained surface. This surface, however, is so fine that there are many thousands of tiny grains to a square inch. Miss Simon does not like to use a soft graphite pencil or a crayon because they clog the space between the grains. When it comes to corrections, only very delicate erasures that do not damage the surface can be successful. A part of the drawing may be scratched out, but cannot then be worked over. Retouching with Chinese white is out, since it does not show on the negative. It is therefore essential when correcting this type of work to limit oneself to additions wherever possible.

Miss Simon has worked for some years to perfect her particular method of planning, finishing, and correcting her preseparated illustrations.

Your hand gets tired from turning the knob in an unsuccessful quest for a worthwhile TV program. You don't want any westerns, spy stories, or soap operas. You are willing to settle for some innocent sports event, and finally find it on an obscure channel.

You are faced with the spectacle of four hefty, long-haired gentlemen in and out of a wrestling ring in a sports arena. The fifth man—the referee—is less muscular, so that every now and then he is belabored by one of the other creatures. There is a great deal of action, excitement—in and out of the ring—and general confusion.

I believe that many of us have been involved at one time or another in similar activities. To be sure, physical wrestling is unusual in publishing offices these days, but what about the situation when an illustrated book "goes into production"?

The participants in this sporting event appear in

this order: (1) the author; (2) the editor; (3) the production manager; (4) the printer; (5)—alas, the designer. It's every man for himself. The author, to be sure, will sometimes team up with the editor, the production manager with the printer. But the production manager might also give secret signals to the editor. Woe to the referee (the designer).

Any book is an intricate thing—even a thing of beauty. While it may have been born out of a spontaneous idea the author had, the more people who get involved in it the less spontaneity it has.

We will not examine here how many people close to the author have infiltrated his sanctum and influenced, helped or hindered him. I remember, gleefully, a dedication which ran: "To my wife and children, without whose help this book would have been finished a year ago."

Like the rings which a pebble thrown into a pond creates, new waves of influence steadily make themselves felt.

If the book is to be illustrated or presents a tricky problem—the production manager is now made a part of one of the innumerable "conferences." Naturally, a production manager has a wide range of experience with illustration and production methods. What is now needed is the blending of the many practical and impractical considerations. This is where the designer comes in—or should come in. It is sad to note that more often than not he is called in after considerable delay, often after illustrative material and even manufacturers have been selected. Now he is to design an attractive book with materials he did not choose or would not have chosen. Any exciting and often perfectly practical ideas he could have contributed come too late to fit into the production scheme of things. To many publishers, even to production managers, the role of a designer is not clear. They usually feel that his talent should enable him to integrate manuscripts and other materials into a more or less prescribed format—to bring order into what sometimes is chaos.

Now consider how much better it would have been to call him in on one of the early conferences. Enthusiastic as a designer usually is, he would have had much to suggest. Some of it would have pleased everyone; some of it would have been rejected for practical reasons. But all the decisions would have been matters of mutual agreement.

I feel very strongly that in the case of an illustrated book, samples suggested by the author should be considered promptly, and not just be accepted eventually because some commitment was made. I could mention many cases in point but will limit myself to one particular instance.

In this case the publisher, a man with little or no experience in printing, had selected as illustrator for a work of fiction a contemporary painter of repute.

He had rather grandly told him to illustrate the book the way he, the painter, saw fit. Quite naturally the artist marched in one day dragging an enormous package containing several large, detailed oil paintings.

At this point a production man was hastily hired. It was his task to get a designer to work with the oil paintings—which were horizontal in shape. A printer, too, had to supply an estimate for the reproduction of the paintings at a cost that would make the publication possible.

Admittedly, this is an extreme case, but as I said before—even in my own limited experience this was not unusual.

Crises in illustrations are provoked by artists whose medium can be reproduced—well—only at great cost or who are unable or unwilling to accept the limitations of a book.

For instance, there is the man or woman who supplies "art" in varying sizes. This usually makes very different rates of reproduction necessary. If the illustrations are for textbooks, often letters or numbers are on the illustrations or have to be added. Or else the artist may have decided to letter some captions and have others set in type. Borders, decorative or not, can make the position of illustrations on the page precarious. Or what about maps which were meant for a double spread but had to go on one page —even sideways—an unfortunate device? Or an illustration or map that is blown up to fit two pages instead of one?

A children's book which I recently designed arrived in my studio in the form of a handful of typewritten pages and sixteen illustrations. I explained to the publisher that it would not make an attractive book in 32 pages: 64 pages, however, seemed ridiculous: 48 pages would be a good possibility, especially if self end papers were considered. No, said the publisher, ends must be in color. Print the whole book in two colors, said I. No, said the publisher, too expensive. Sixty-four pages it had to be, as the book was to be printed in one color and had to be sold at a rather high price. The outcome was to have each illustration backed by a blank page which gave the book—admittedly—a feeling of being padded.

One of the first questions I had asked was whether the artist would do a few more illustrations. A laconic "No" came over the wire, but I know that a more detailed answer would be: "The artist did not get very much for the artwork" or, "The artist has gone to Greece or Paris." A joint conference could have straightened out this minor problem in a very brief time.

Artists, naturally, trust a designer to be fair and reasonable more than they do other members of a publishing house. Still, the publisher doesn't want us to get too chummy and have the designer make concessions and allowances. Very often the artists are lured by an author friend or have the naïve hope that illustrating books is easy and/or profitable and may be good publicity. There is an atmosphere of little tolerance and little understanding on both sides. All this, of course, applies mostly to dealings with newcomers, but it is astounding how many times some publishers are involved in such situations. Could it be low-cost planning?

In the planning of textbooks, another element comes to the foreground. Some textbooks require a tremendous number and variety of illustrations. These are drawn illustrations, photographs, historical pictures, maps, diagrams, etc. Where to get them in a few months? It becomes necessary to tap all available sources. Naturally, money is the main object. When you work with hundreds of illustrations, you cannot pay heavy fees for reproduction rights on more than some of them. The rest come out of the New York Public Library, Picture Division, and from many sources.

My concern here is not how the material is obtained or what it costs, but how it can be integrated without tears.

When a large quantity of drawings, some in line, others with wash, are used together, with lines of varying thickness, all liberally decorated with much type—all different, to be sure—you must first take a deep breath. Perhaps some may be weeded out, some type may be reset, some drawings retouched. All is not lost—yet. It is astonishing how such a book may still look decent, not like an old mail-order catalog. This must be left up to the designer's ingenuity. The layouts with their interplay of black and white can rescue a hodge-podge of unstylish "art." Sometimes a very bold typographic approach helps—sometimes using tint blocks, or screening line illustrations to convert them from black to gray.

Generally speaking, I am for democratic design-production conferences with editors sitting in and not for dictatorial laws laid down by the production department's notoriously hard-boiled and not very sensitive aesthetic reasoning.

Much confusion and excitement could be avoided if the production manager were informed at the earliest possible moment of the publisher's intention to sign a contract. He could then, either with his own experience or with the help of a designer or printer, prepare a memo that would give the author clear guidelines. To be sure, the author would get much less leeway, and he might conceivably complain about being hamstrung. In the end, however, he would recognize that it would be in his favor to have books clearly planned, designed, and produced.

There is room for all points of view—what the authors and editors would like the book to be, and what the designer wants it to look like. The schedules, commitments, and costs—all concerns of the ever-watchful production department—have to be integrated parts of the plan, too.

Naturally, there will be disagreements, dark hints about champagne taste with beer money, minor hysteria, but eventually a new stylish, glossy book will be on your desk when you have given up expecting it. By then you are involved with at least one other book in production and with still another or two in the planning stage. "Sorry," says the telephone operator, "they are *all* in conference!"

Recently I had occasion to browse through a number of illustrated books. Actually I am referring to books illustrated with photographs. The textbooks and how-to-do-it books presented a very different picture, of course, from those in which the illustrations were paramount.

Sometimes the illustrations were background to the text, sometimes the text became an extended caption to the illustrations. On a number of quite different occasions I have been involved in the design of books of the latter type; there has often been a dramatic quality to such involvement.

The war in Korea was still raging when a very large package arrived at my desk. Opening it I found a short manuscript and a big collection of photographic prints. It was quite obvious that the prints were blown up from 35mm film as the enlargements still showed the sprocket holes. I looked at the prints for a while, having no information on the proposed book. When I discussed the manuscript and illustrations with the production manager he was rather vague. Nobody knew much about the material except that the book had been accepted and was to be published under the title *The Face of War*. The photographs consisted entirely of enlargements of film taken by two young photographers in the front-line position and more than once during battles. The photographers had selected the illustrations they thought most dramatic and had written a text around them. The design and production problem was twofold. First of all, we would have to limit the number of pictures without impairing the powerful impact they had, being careful not to eliminate any that were described in the text. Out of the remaining material I would have to develop photographic sequences maintaining a change of speed which is so characteristic of war.

The second problem was that of the quality of the print. On first examination the prints looked very bad. They seemed to be very badly scratched. I guessed that something had happened to the film while it was in the camera, but I never found out exactly what. The production manager looked doubtfully at the prints.

"Perhaps we should get them retouched," he suggested, with a resigned expression.

I explained to him that this could cost a great deal of time and money. He decided to talk to the photographers and authors of the book. Perhaps he believed that they felt it would be in the interest of an attractive book to get the illustrations prettied up. Eventually, I persuaded him that the face of war could not be pretty, but would be scratched to say the least and that, in fact, the illustrations were entirely unposed and authentic.

I suggested, therefore, that we use the photographic material exactly as it was, and proceeded immediately to lay out the book. As the text was brief I was able to obtain rough galley proofs very quickly and after determining an acceptable number of pages, I could begin to work with the illustrations.

No one interfered with me. My layouts were rough but fell into a pattern which to me seemed proper for the material photographed and described. The same 35mm frames supplied several small action pictures on one page as they were blown up to full pages and even double spreads. I believe that I succeeded in reproducing what the young cameramen had experienced and intended to convey. I finally met them shortly after the book was printed. They were very pleased, in particular with the fact that none of their pictures had been retouched.

"Vergogna," cried Arturo Toscanini. "Shame on you! The violin must *sing!*"

A few years ago the Vanguard Press was in the process of publishing the warm-hearted account of *This Was Toscanini* by Samuel Antek, violinist in Toscanini's NBC Symphony Orchestra. It seemed obvious that this book should be illustrated. Rarely has there been a more photogenic man than Arturo Toscanini. Portraits and miscellaneous photographs were probably available from different sources but they did not seem right. However, Vanguard struck it rich, learning that a substantial quantity of candid photographs of Toscanini had been made by an ardent admirer of the conductor's art, Robert Hupka. It was then that I was asked to design *This Was Toscanini.*

I was in on this book from the very beginning— which is what one always wants and rarely accomplishes. Had I known then the amount of work, heartache and, oh yes, pleasure that were involved in the designing of this book, I might have settled for doing the jacket only.

When I arrived at Vanguard's office I was shown a big pile of photographs, all of them equally substantial in size and thickness, and was introduced to the man who had taken them.

Robert Hupka had had the good fortune of being present at many of the *Maestro's* recording sessions. While the orchestra rehearsed and Toscanini begged, wheedled, and threatened, to get all the best from their instruments, Hupka managed to photograph all he saw. He took more than 1500 photographs, most of them on a 35mm Leica (equipped with a tele-lens), and a few on a Speed Graphic. He had made innumerable prints of each frame he had taken. Every exposure was carefully catalogued and filed. He never allowed anyone else to use his negatives.

I was overwhelmed by the beauty of the pictures as well as by their sheer number. Photographically speaking, every grain of the emulsion had been accounted for. We blew them up to many times original size—a print ½ inch wide was blown up to twelve inches, a ¼ inch print to five inches, and so on. Yet no detail was lost.

Over one hundred of these photographs were now lying in front of me. I looked at the publisher. "Are all of these going in?" I inquired. "How many pages do you expect to make? Do you have any idea of the trim size? How much will the book sell for? How many copies will you print?"

Both the publisher and Mr. Hupka seemed bewildered. I pursued my advantage. Without waiting very long for an answer, I told them how *I* visualized the book. There was discussion but no disagreement. I had won the first round.

Sample pages were set in a routine manner. I obtained from Mr. Hupka some prints, cropped them and arranged them with text—for which I had chosen Palatino—in an eight-page dummy. When he saw the dummy he was not happy. I had cropped "his pictures!" Perhaps encouraged by my initial success, I had forgotten that every square inch of black background on a photograph is as dear to a photographer as all of the canvas is to a painter.

I decided then and there that it would be best to work directly *with* him. There would be no conflict with the author as he had died two or three years before. As for the publisher, she very wisely let me fight my own battles.

It would be difficult to review the many days and long evenings of putting photographs on our living room floor, and laying out pages, invariably double spreads. Time and time again the photographer and I looked over his material. Every print was as dear to him as an only child and he had hundreds of them which had already been weeded out of a far greater number. I could not but admire his ability and tenacity. We argued and we agreed, we engaged in horse trading, we threatened and cajoled each other, but it was all in a good cause.

During my many sessions with Hupka, I learned many things. I believe a designer can profit from the unorthodox approach of one who is not a designer. There was no question about his intense familiarity with every one of the hundreds of prints we considered. Aside from his very definite ideas on which illustrations would fit a sequence of the manuscript (remember, the photos and the manuscript had not had any connection with each other originally), he would remember virtually all the shots he had taken. He could identify the needed material rapidly. He explained everything that had gone on in the studio, every gesture of the great conductor whose stamina outlasted that of most of his musicians.

Occasionally, I tried to have my way with layouts which seemed proper to me, but it was here that Mr. Hupka's stamina came to the fore. I know that I talked *him* out of some horrible photomontages, but I also know that he talked *me* into doing things with photographs I didn't want to do. All the same, the result spoke for itself. When I had first looked at the photographs I had immediately seen layouts before me. Only now did I become conscious of the artistic quality of the photographs. It is obvious that in a book about one man, always doing the same thing, but with even an endless variation of expressions, one could easily tire of the inevitable black background, the little man with the white mustache, and the men at their music stands.

The problem, therefore, was to dramatize and co-ordinate the very lively account with the photographs available. It may seem ironic that even with 1500 photographs, occasionally we did not have quite the right one.

I have said before that Mr. Hupka did not like his pictures to be cropped. Actually, some were cropped a great deal. This was wherever it seemed important to have a number of photographs on the same page, in order to illustrate a certain passage in the text. They might be followed by full-size illustrations and occasionally by a grandiose double spread, bleeding all four sides. I have always felt that one of the most important things in a book with many photographs is a change of speed, preferably in the nature of the photo itself, but if necessary by means of cropping and changing of size.

At the very beginning of the production of *This Was Toscanini* we had talked a great deal about sheet-fed photogravure. However, it was doubtful if the publisher could afford this. So we switched our talk to offset. We had a number of samples made using the same photograph and we realized soon enough that we would not be satisfied with offset. Ironically, in its German version, the book was reproduced by offset and looked very poor by comparison—ironically, because it is so often assumed that all European printing is better than the domestic product.

One of the most dramatic photographs was used for the jacket. I dared to omit title and author from the front cover, putting them only on the backbone. It was my contention that no one passing a bookstore could resist looking at that amazing face, and that those who didn't know whom it depicted would probably want to find out. The book was entirely printed in black with a warm brownish tinge. The end papers were grayish blue.

Typographically there were no bad problems with the book until a listing of recordings, which would be of great interest to record collectors, was appended. This listing, in a size considerably smaller than that of the text, had to be coordinated so that it wouldn't jar the nerves of the gentle reader.

Designers rarely keep time sheets and none were kept for this job. Eventually, the book was published and everybody was highly pleased. It made the "Fifty Books" and received an international award at the Frankfurt Book Fair.

Although I am horrified by war, in *The Face of War* I had been able to reproduce it graphically. Although I am in love with art and music, I found myself all but drained when my layouts went to the printer.

Instinctively I used in both books a change-of-pace technique. I know that I did not look at that book while I was designing *Toscanini* but now that I can compare them, certain comparisons are inevitable. There are the double spreads, full pages and numbers of small illustrations on the page. The texts are set in different type faces, but the style is unmistakably the same; it is the accompaniment to the melody of illustrations.

Designing *The Face of War* had a quality of a dramatic, almost impetuous dress rehearsal, whereas *This Was Toscanini* turned out to be a polished command performance.

QR

Part Five: Life in the Industry

ST

Time and events

move faster and faster—it seems—but it is to be hoped that thoughts will not become obsolete like fashions or electronic equipment.

True, obsolescence in our industry is not quite the same thing as it is elsewhere. The same men who, quite naturally, prefer to "jet" there in half the time (or less), the same women who must rush to the stores for longer or shorter skirts or different shoes, they all will open a book of some sort at one time or another.

Perhaps it is a thirty-five cent pocket book, perhaps a $20 art book, perhaps a novel for $5.95. It will consist of so many signatures of paper, sewn and cased in bookcloth or perfect bound and cased in stiff paper. It may fit into your pocket or else on your coffee table. But it will be a book.

Technology is a wonderful thing. We are promised that before long we will be able to receive over the air virtually any book that was ever published. That is to say, it will be as easy to read books as to turn on your favorite TV program.

I wonder whether this means that more people will read more books; they cannot very well read a book while watching a western on TV. I wonder what books will become "best readers."

It does seem very easy, but I fear that the easier technology makes it for us, the less we will appreciate what a book can offer to us.

When I was a youngster I built a little radio with a crystal detector, a radio based on a simple blueprint that was then available to me. What an experience it was when the clumsy little set worked!

Other experiences that were grand but not easily accomplished were my first visits to the theater, the opera, and for that matter, the race track. In these cases, I was naturally taken along by my parents or brothers, but each time it took a good deal of preparation and effort.

Today, much less effort is needed. A youngster is placed before a TV set, given a peanut butter-and-jelly sandwich, and the rest is easy. But does he enjoy the program half as much as I enjoyed my experiences?

Will we enjoy reading books on a screen? Will we not miss finding or receiving a book, holding it in our hands, opening it, thumbing a little through the pages and then resolutely turning to page 1? Do we not enjoy rereading a page that has fascinated us particularly, or even falling asleep with the open book on our lap? Personally, I believe the book is here to stay, no matter what technology will do, just as wooden furniture is somehow more agreeable to the touch than plastic.

We all know Tolstoy's wonderful story: *How much land does a man want?* As much as he can walk from dawn to dusk in a square. He starts full of energy and hoping to measure for himself a substantial plot. By midmorning he turns the first corner, always careful to stake out his claim. At noon, he should be halfway he figures, but he sees a lovely field and can't pass it up. When he finally rounds his second corner it is well past noon, at the third he sees the sun going down toward the fields. He hurries, but long before he can get back to the starting point he drops from exhaustion—dead. He is buried in a plot, six feet deep, six feet long, three feet wide. This is all the land he needs.

How much for a book? How much care, attention to the details of design, composition, presswork, binding? How long should one have marveled at the wonder of paper? How young was one when one set the first type? How much did one learn about type faces, design, typefitting, suitability? How many cloth samples has one looked at critically, comparing subtle color variations? How many men and women in the book industry did one get to know, how many of their plants did one visit? How many books did one read? How much for a book?

This morning I found myself on the "eight o'clock" (New Haven) commuter train. It was whittled down from five to three cars so half of us were standing in heavy overcoats as it was freezing outside. The rest were sitting down with chattering teeth, for the train was not heated.

As it crawled toward New York with the patient, unperturbed tenacity of a caterpillar, I tried to reconcile the complete deterioration of a once-proud railroad with the price of a dinner in an average restaurant—enough to do a complete grocery shopping tour for two in former years.

There are so many parallels to this situation that I don't need to put them down, but they all leave the big question mark: Do prosperity and decay have to go together? What is it that prevents us from printing and binding books as well with our mile-long modern machinery as we did (or could) half a century ago?

Why should good typography be limited to fine presses and to some prestige books. Why all these high, impressive prices, and so little that one could call tasteful, modest, economical in means and material? Why does there seem to be a general decline, an apathy, in short, a lack of imagination? As Rosa Dottle in *David Copperfield* says, "I would be happy to have an answer, I would like to know."

The point I am making is that a craft ought not to be allowed to deteriorate to the level of pure commercialism. Heaven knows there are people in most fields of endeavor, including the book industry, who are not at all concerned with what they produce, but only with its financial returns. "But," they say, "it sells!" Which sounds to me suspiciously like the famous quotation, "The public be damned!"

Half a millennium has passed since Johann Gutenberg hit upon, experimented with, and finally made practical, the use of movable printing types. By the standards of his day the invention was tremendously practical. It obviated the need to dictate a book to a group of calligraphers seated in a small room, a process which was costly and time-consuming. To be sure, each book, or manuscript as we call it, would be appreciated and treasured, certainly not gather dust or perhaps even be remaindered. Today we are using high speed typesetting machinery and fast presses and we have further cut the cost and time for the production of books.

Yet today, the forty-two line Bible that came off Johann Gutenberg's press is still considered one of the most beautiful books ever printed and is, of course, invaluable. The question, then, of it being an example of practical printing may be considered irrelevant. Paper plates and plastic mixing bowls, too, are more practical than china and earthenware but not likely to be admired or remembered long.

Much has been said of the transition from printer/ designer to printers and designers. It has been pointed out that in the rapid industrial growth, machinery more and more took the place of personal skill. Setting by machine created incredible speed but did away with typographic understanding. A machine operator today is a highly skilled typist with a sufficient knowledge of his machine, be it a Linotype or a Monotype, seldom both.

There is, of course, now a production department (supposedly) with enough taste and skill to specify exactly how books are to be manufactured to be attractive. Inside and free-lance book designers are available for this specific task. Some books are designed well, others not. Some are veritable coffee table masterpieces, so glorious that one shies away from opening them more than once—others go through production entirely innocent of design. Many books, allegedly "designed," exhibit little imagination. Limited by format, these books often rely on the supposed eye-appeal photographic illustrations offer (in color and/or black and white). The whole package is then wrapped in dust jackets that shine like cheap china under a strong light.

Now, granted that we want to make books attractive for the reader, to stimulate his interest in the book, and for that matter to attract the prospective buyer. But just what is enough design, not too much, not too little?

Design-conscious as I quite naturally am, I do realize how little I care about the design if the subject matter of the book is of great concern to me. Books should not be an integral part of furniture, never to be opened, but on the other hand, they could be something better than just tools in the garage.

Doctors, lawyers, just about all professional people have a working library which looks businesslike and is being used, but does not mix well with the typical art book, fiction, or even sets of classics.

I believe a book to be a living thing, one that can outlive men, families, nations. I am making a plea for books that are not dressed up, not neglected, but for books that are of the best material suitable and of lasting quality. They will have a simple beauty that is not man-made—or at least it will not seem so.

As in so many things, planning ahead is essential for quality here, too. Discuss the book with the designer even before you actually have it. Line up the manufacturer. Check your paper inventory. Look at competing books or at least at your own production of the last season. Consider suitable type faces.

Many of the men and women who are responsible for the production of books do make an effort to arrange for tasteful and thoughtful design, for sound materials—even if they must be of a modest quality —and for faultless production. In order to insure these efforts, greatest care should be given to a fair schedule, not one dictated to the manufacturers but worked out with them.

Unfortunately many sins have been committed in

the name of unforeseen emergencies which might have easily been anticipated. Thus there is a good deal of mutual distrust between publishers and manufacturers. But show us any two groups, small or large, and dependent upon each other, who will not fight in some manner. The book industry with its many groups of varying purposes is no exception. However, it should be noted here that ways and means are forever being discussed to remedy this situation.

A word about the position of production manager. Self-made men and women abound. Many have started as office boys or typists. Some of them have made the very best production managers I know, but such a beginning coupled with a lack of cultural background is not exactly a prerequisite of brilliance. I suspect that many owe their deserved or undeserved position to a management tendency to economize on the production staff. It could be that this tendency can cost the publisher more than he saves on annual salaries! I have seen that happen more than once. As the book industry pays less than "Madison Avenue" it must take those who are less competent and hope for a fair share of idealists who are in "publishing" because they prefer it, at the cost of being less affluent.

The plucky mayor of the city of New York, Fiorello La Guardia, often urged: "Patience and Fortitude!" What could be more appropriate? In much the same way, a European publisher whose memory is very dear to me, said often: "One has to have courage to be a publisher!" He also showed me the true meaning of patience, and moreover, his appreciation of some of the work I was able to do for him was genuine and even now fills me with pleasure. His memory has done much to help me overcome a deep aversion to some (very few—thank God) people in our industry whose insolence is only topped by their ignorance. How do they keep their jobs?

Whoever found the solution to untying the Gordian knot would be busy indeed untying the knotty network of book manufacturing these days. I remember being faced at one time with the problem of how to deal with a set of galley proofs in which practically no paragraph had escaped the red fountain pen of our final reader. Were we to make *some* corrections? All of them? Or, perhaps reset the whole book, which I was assured would cost more than all those AA's, as author's alterations are called. The publisher was called, the publisher called the author, the author called her husband (at his Wall Street office) and he cut the Gordian knot. He simply decreed to disregard the proofreader's red marks entirely, and to print the book as is (or *was*, I suppose). Frankly, I admired him!

The other day I came across an old schedule for the production of a book. This schedule in itself was no mean achievement. It was articulate if unrealistic. It required utmost strain and accomplishment from publisher, author, designer, manufacturer and, of course, from everyone connected with them. It was truly a tour de force. Were it not, unfortunately, likely that:

1) several components would not "come through" and 2) that in the end the publishing event would probably misfire with a very little "pouf," I would have been as enthusiastic about the schedule as its author.

On an ill-fated Friday in April of 1945 I was sitting in a bus in New York, when I noticed a strange general commotion on Herald Square. The windows of the bus were open and I heard unusual shouting. A woman in the bus wept openly. In another moment I knew President Roosevelt had suddenly died.

That same evening, still numb from the awful shock, I received a telephone call from the editor of the (original) Pocket Books, Donald Geddes. He asked me to come to his office Saturday morning. This was very unusual but he was urgent and short. I decided to go.

In his office the next day he told me that Pocket Books was that very moment compiling a memorial volume to FDR and that he wanted me to design it.

Textual material was being compiled by editors, news commentators, agencies, etc. Pictorial material would reach me in the afternoon. By evening the half-ready material would be sent by messenger to Clinton, Massachusetts, to be set by the Colonial Press that night.

I settled down to the rather simple but horrid task of designing a manuscript I had not even seen. I had no idea of its length, the nature of its chapters, titles, etc. By midafternoon things began to fall into place. Donald Geddes, Bill Gleason (then the "man in the New York Office"), and I took a train to Clinton.

Sunday was spent in simultaneous proofreading, designing, and typesetting. Engravings and pages were made up, captions were inserted at the very last minute. Plates had to be made and curved, as the book would be run on a perfecting rotary press. I fell asleep in the composing room watching the stone men work as late as two o'clock Monday morning.

The presses had begun to run, the rolls of paper got smaller and were replaced again and again. I walked up to the floor above where the unending sheets came up through the floor; were rolled into the (then new) perfect binding machinery; folded, gathered, inserted two up in a preprinted cover by George Salter; glued in and trimmed. There they were, one after another, in an unending stream.

There were 60,000 or more printed over the weekend. The Press had truly done all they could. The publisher saw to it that the books would be on the stands that very day.

Now this was an extraordinary accomplishment, achieved without the benefit of any schedule simply because no one had time to devise one.

The unattainable, the unrealistic is often pictured in your unconscious in a dream—or even in a more or less deliberate daydream. Your memories, too, have a way of gilding tarnished frames, of freshening faded pictures. In short the dream world has much to recommend itself.

All the same, we live in a very real world, hardly "the stuff that dreams are made of." Can we still get pleasure and satisfaction out of what we are doing? There is a wide range from the old pro who knows his production or stock or customers, to whom all this seemingly means just dollars and cents, to the young (or old) student who sets type for a four page booklet, selects paper and prints for the sheer delight of it.

Just as hardly a day goes by when I don't learn something new in this world of paper and lead, they, too, all of them, learn all the time. But many are finished at four-thirty or five; some worry, eat, dream printing and find themselves frequently discouraged. Even if they are not overly concerned with the tangible rewards, they have somehow never fallen in love with printing, with paper and with books.

While it is true that there is usually not too much time to ponder the finished job, as the new one requires all your attention, a man should know it if he has finished a work of art. And art it is, no matter how little or how much goes into it. Call it skill if you like or find a more suitable word for it, but don't pass up the moment when your accomplishment is waiting to be inspected. If too much has gone wrong, you can say: "Well, in all, it is handsome. The paper is good, the presswork fine. Can I, or we, improve on it the next time?" Usually there is room for improvement; usually it means more organization in the publishing house, more application by the designer, more patience by the printer.

In that year the Christmas party at the book manufacturing plant I worked for as designer fell on a Thursday, the day before Christmas Eve. There would be a half-day of work on Friday. For some of us it would be a half-hearted activity; for the people in the plant there would be more Christmas parties and more liquor. Work would start up slowly again the following Monday.

The office party was held in a little waiting room next to the telephone operator's switchboard. Things were getting fairly chummy. Unappealing secretaries were sitting on the knees of their hitherto unapproachable superiors. Son of the boss came in and smiled winningly at one and all. A great little family.

At this point I caught the eye of the telephone operator, who motioned me over to her cage. "The boss wants you right away," she whispered to me. It was almost like a spy movie routine. I was puzzled, the more so as I had had very few dealings with him and I couldn't help thinking that perhaps he wanted to give me a bonus personally. However, this was in the 1930's and therefore the thought was preposterous.

As I walked down the long corridor leading to the inner sanctum, I noticed some other men from various departments walking down in much the same quiet, bewildered manner. One of them even held onto a highball but he was advised to leave it outside in the hall. Perhaps he wanted to drink to the health of the boss. I was sure by now that we could not all expect bonuses. By the time we entered the private office and stood on the carpet in a half-circle before the decorative desk behind which the boss was comfortably seated, I realized that this was an emergency.

Beside and slightly behind the boss, stood his tall, good-looking private secretary. She had not been taking part in the Christmas party and she looked grave. At a sign from him she produced a telegram and read a statement from a customer who requested finished books by Monday, the 27th. The book in question was a bilingual classic play to be printed in two colors and bound in a rather fussy binding, for which I was responsible. The book was illustrated by a man very much in vogue in those years.

There was silence all around. Everyone realized that the job had been shamefully neglected. Because the book was bilingual, and for some other technical reasons, no one had made any particular effort to push it along and, since the publisher himself liked to travel to faraway places, his absence had caused more delays.

It was not unlike the situation in which people have been invited for dinner long ago and when they show up at the appointed hour the hosts have forgotten all about it and there is nary a frankfurter in the house, to say nothing of drinks and cheese dips.

The boss spoke up with the severity which was his hallmark. You couldn't help but feel little when he addressed you, which was not often. I remember well the group of key people, most of them in their shirt-sleeves—I had quickly slipped on my jacket to receive my bonus—who were standing like so many felons in a police line-up.

What was wanted of us was made abundantly clear: We were to produce a few thousand copies of the book on Christmas Eve, Christmas day and the Sunday after Christmas. Normally it would have taken at least three weeks, working very hard.

I was the only one-man department. I did not need any machinery. Tracing paper, pencils, pica ruler and our type books were my tools. But all the others had to have men to set type, to haul paper, to mix ink, to run presses, to fold sheets, to collate signatures, to sew books, to round them, back them, glue them, stain them, trim them, and case them in. And the cases had to be prepared, too, the boards cut, the cloth slit, cases made, the binding design stamped— in two colors and gold. For this purpose, binding dies had to be routed and finished by an outside company who might take a dim view of working on Christmas Eve. The jackets had to be printed in two or three colors and, before you could say Jack Robinson, the book might be finished.

I don't know how many man-hours of overtime it took. No matter whose fault it may have been, the various unions saw to it that double time was paid on Sundays and holidays, but at least some of the books, perhaps the first hundred copies, were delivered first thing Monday morning by an unhappy trucker complete with hangover.

The account was saved. It was, and remained, a very small account, and eventually it broke away from us anyway and found new suppliers. I don't believe that the publisher knows to this day what happened, and most of the principals in this story are either dead or retired. The author of the book certainly has been for many years.

This is what service a customer could expect in those days. The tables are turned now and I am a little sorry that "the boss" did not live to see the day when he would be implored to take on a job and when time and money didn't matter. Well, didn't matter much.

I'm for free enterprise and a middle-of-the-roader. I don't like to hear people grovel, whether they be customers or suppliers.

"The estimate (or the proofs) went out this morning."

"We had some trouble with the folding equipment."

"I didn't know you wanted it this week (month, year, what have you?)."

Does it all sound familiar to you? On the other hand, there is "Could you come right over?", "We must have it tomorrow.", "Why does it take so long?"

The less I say about this, the better. I don't want to be lynched! But couldn't something be worked out that would be fair to both sides? I have always tried to work with, and not for, customers. Conversely, I have not made unreasonable requests—at least I don't think so. My experience is, if you don't press people unduly and if you can withstand pressure, you last a lot longer in this industry.

One way in which this can be accomplished, in my opinion, is to make a proper effort to acquaint yourself with the working methods and the amount of time required by the various stages of book design and book production. Don't just let the salesman take you out for lunch, but visit his plant as well.

How long does it take a linotype operator to set a galley of type of simple copy such as fiction or biography? Find out how much time it takes (on a pro rata basis) to proof the type that comes from the machine, to proofread it and for the operator to correct it. You are not charged for these "office corrections" but they take time. Watch a man at the stone page a somewhat complicated textbook, go to the press room and stay with them through the first "make-ready." Interest yourself in a hydraulic press which is used to stamp covers with metal or pigment foil. Watch it being set up.

In fact, allow at least a morning or an afternoon to see each major department in a book manufacturing concern, (a composing room, a foundry, a pressroom, or a bindery). In between, the salesman will take you out to lunch anway. Find out what offset, color separation, photoengraving, and gravure processes are. Though you may never get a chance to use his skills, go to a hand binder and admire his craft— which is much older than printing itself.

My Latin teacher, who was given to quoting liberally from the classics, liked to say, "Well, Salter, let us not forget the great times in which we live, over the minor annoyances (homework, of course) of the day." I wonder if this trite saying cannot be turned upside down and inside out to read: "Even though we live in such horrible times, let us have some fun occasionally, like—you guessed it—a nice job of printing. Instead, it sometimes seems as if the following is a common dialogue in a plant's executive offices.

Q. Do we have the machinery to do good work?

A. Yes.

Q. Then why, in the name of St. Waysgoose, don't we?

Pick your own answer from these:

A. 1. "The customer wouldn't know the difference." 2. "It doesn't pay." 3. "Never thought of it."

When I was designer for one book manufacturer in New York, I offered to take any one of the office staff for a plant tour to acquaint him with the work we were doing. My offer was almost unanimously declined. They just were not interested in what I considered the far-more interesting side of the business. There were a few exceptions, and those who took an interest in production have since advanced in the "trade" and hold better positions than they would have dreamed of then.

Presumably there are readers who have been exposed to the challenging life in book manufacturing and design where $2 \times 2 = 5$ and where sorcery has to be practiced as a means to an end.

Perhaps the following account will therefore amuse those in production who have recently been subjected to another one of those economy drives.

At the occasion of a rather large meeting of the

industry a very famous industrial designer was asked how he went about book design problems. He answered that his studio would send one or two of his assistants to the offices of the publisher to acquaint themselves with his production procedures, house style, etc. They would then conduct pertinent research experiments—and eventually come up with facts and recommendations at which point he would take over. No one in this audience was bold enough to ask what his fee might be.

I have often thought that nothing much happens at most of these meetings. True, it is nice to renew old acquaintances over a saucer of melting ice cream with cookies and in many cases the tab is picked up by someone with an expense account. Still, the participants in these culinary forums rarely come to grips with the pressing problems which beset them morning and afternoon pretty much every day of the week. If more publishers and editors and fewer suppliers were at these meetings the discussions would be more open and more informative and therefore profitable. Everyone else is pretty familiar with most of these problems as they have been aired these thirty years.

The quality and cost problem as well as that of proper scheduling will not be solved by cutting corners or by hiring inexperienced personnel. Quality of production and true economy can only be achieved by persons of proven ability and reliability.

Where manufacturers will not take pride in workmanship and where they welcome newer methods only when they are forced upon them, the social graces of their representatives can not cover up a cynical approach to the art and craft of printing.

A rare final edition with a single page printed upside down and a United States airmail stamp of yesteryear with its center printed upside down have this in common: Their value can be immense—not because printing upside down is a virtue but because it is not happening often—thank God! On the other hand, to be upside down is essential to the pineapple upside-down cake.

I happen to be interested in all the above-mentioned articles. In the case of the book, I am fascinated by its faulty improvision. I feel the printer was called away or busy daydreaming. In regard to the stamp, I wish I owned it, as its value has gone up quite miraculously from twelve cents to $50,000.

As for the cake, it makes good eating, or as an Indian guide in Alaska said: "Good biting!" What is it, then, that makes a defect so valuable in our eyes? In the case of the stamp it is a rarity which the collector regards with the same affection that the owner of a painting by a Master will feel: That it is absolutely one of a kind. In the case of the book it may indicate the first edition, the error presumably having been found and removed from subsequent editions.

The schooled eye will find some fault in most books; if it is a glaring error it is likely to be removed, of course. It may be a comfort to those who have admitted—if only to themselves—having caused such errors here and there, that the Navajo Indians believed it to be wrong for human beings to be perfect. This they reasoned was reserved for their gods. Consequently their sand paintings and their rugs usually showed some small surprising imperfection.

I doubt that our designers or binders or printers have similar examples. What mistakes are made come quite naturally, nor are they likely to be accompanied by an apology. This goes under the "We're only human" department.

A large group of people from the book industry meet for a day's outing and a gay picnic—nothing formal, no speeches, no exhibits, no dinners or round-table discussions leading nowhere—just fun. Just friends getting together. Still I overheard the following dialogue:

"You won't believe it, but they left two and a half pages blank in our last book—in the middle!"

"I can top that! Our printers set one line of each title on the contents page in 12 point and the runover in 14 point." "Why, do you suppose?" "Well— our designers had marked 12/14 Baskerville."

"I can top that," (triumphantly). "Our printers left folios on *all* front matter pages, exchanged the card page and copyright pages and—started each of fourteen index pages with the same big sinkage and INDEX in display!" "Don't they have proofreaders?" "I guess so, but they were in an awful hurry!" "Don't *you* have editors?" "Yes, but they are away in Europe or someplace."

I wandered away and thought how nothing new ever happens.

Most people who read books are part of a grand testing program. Even the young ones give books a substantial workout. If they can't tear it, it can't be torn. In the school bus population in this country there is a sizable percentage dedicated to testing the strength of the binding (boards, cloth, thread, paste, and all) by throwing textbooks the length of the bus. Many books are said to survive this test, not all.

Once grown up, those of the reading population who also smoke usually have a matchbook handy to mark their page. Nonsmokers by and large have to stay with the tried and true device of turning the corner of such pages. If the book does not open easily, a determined reader can arrange for it to remain open permanently.

Now it is true that some of the more cynical publishers reason that such books can be replaced when their appearance is disgraceful, but can one count on that? Since even a concerted effort to educate the reading public to gentleness in the handling of books is not likely to be successful, why don't we make

204 FROM COVER TO COVER

stronger bindings? By that I mean *not* side stitched bindings, but stronger thread (nylon?), better boards and cloth. I am inviting someone to invent a method of making the casebound book as strong (well almost as strong) as the bound book.

Many of us are aware that the hitherto prohibitive cost of gilding (by hand with gold leaf) has been bridged by a gilding machine which can apply a tarnish-resistant roll gold to the tops of books. I certainly would welcome seeing some books in richer bindings. The price differential might be anywhere from five to fifteen cents and I know that is a lot for bindings and means an increase of twenty-five to seventy-five cents, but wouldn't we love to see and buy finer editions bound in a buckram cloth with headbands and gilt top and cheerfully pay an additional dollar if it was a book dear to us, or more likely, a birthday or Christmas gift?

Some of these books—particularly during the Christmas season—might be displayed at great advantage minus a gaudy jacket and wrapped in acetate, if the publisher were proud of the binding. I feel the bookstores might welcome such an innovation. After all, they, too, are very conscious of the display value of books as they cannot depend on only the sales of the current best sellers, cards, and paperbacks.

Not so very long ago I became interested not only in the designing, but also in the planning, of a series of books on recreation and related fields. I redesigned some titles that had been done years ago, but were still in print; I used the old material where possible, and designed new titles.

In discussing plans for the new books in the series, I pointed out that a certain title published several years earlier seemed to me to be obsolete. I felt that it would be wise to commission a suitable person to write a new book on the same topic. It had something to do with camping. The concept of camping it represented was old-fashioned, the illustrations showed Boy Scouts wearing the old-style "campaign hats," and the terminology in the book was easily four decades old.

To produce a new manuscript on the subject, the publisher approached a Boy Scout leader, a young man who had been an Eagle Scout and was now scoutmaster in a suburban community. He was also a junior executive in a publishing house. He seemed enthusiastic about the project and promised to consider the assignment, though he was extremely busy. What would make his participation particularly desirable was his talent for drawing; he would be able to supply up-to-date sketches of all aspects of camping.

I inquired every six weeks or so about the progress of our project. When a year or two had gone past and no promise to do the book had been made by him, and no other author had been found, I asked again. I told the publisher that, although I was, myself, not especially interested in camping, I truly felt that the very existence of this outdated book was a liability.

The publisher looked at me, smiling faintly, and said, "Funny that you should mention that book. It is really one of our most successful titles. We reprint it more than once a year."

Could it be that the obsolete has a romantic appeal, that old handbooks are desirable as antiques? Perhaps this will open new vistas in publishing and design.

When we consider that the design and production of any given book might be *with the times* or *behind the times*, inevitably it would seem best to create a format that is *ahead of the times*. This is particularly desirable because the preparation, design, and production of such books take a great deal of time, effort, and money. To be "behind the times" would be fatal, if only because the competition would get a welcome edge in the field. To be merely "with the times" quite naturally dates the book, for, by the time the books come from the binder, many improvements may have been made.

It stands to reason, then, that one should be "ahead of the times." This, however, is easier said than done. For one thing, a bold, new approach with which the designer has familiarized himself could easily shock his publisher. The reason for this is obvious, a good designer lives and dreams design all the time. He might come up with new, stunning approaches, even practical ones from a production point of view. On the other hand, the publisher, his editors, production people, and sales staff have other problems with which they live. Therefore, an entirely new concept might be welcomed by them but not without an initial gasp. When things settle down a bit, and the designer has explained his reasons for doing what he is doing, and the production people are beginning to admit that the mechanics do not present insurmountable difficulties, the editors will probably warm up to the idea too. Now comes the most difficult task—the sales department must be convinced that, even if "the boat is being rocked," substantial advantages, such as increased sales, can be assumed to result from the proposed drastic changes.

It is true that it would be easier to try such ideas on individual books in one field or another, but, where less is at stake, there is also proportionately less interest in such changes. Here the slogan "let George do it" often applies. It has been my experience that the big publishers would indicate a hope for the smaller publishers to go ahead with such ideas to "create a market." The small publishers in turn, point to the affluence of the larger publisher compared with their own financial problems.

Sooner or later, someone will inevitably do what you have wanted to do for some time. I have sometimes felt that my innermost ideas were copied or that I gave them away inadvertently. Actually, such ideas are "in the air." It is just a question of who sees them first as attractive, applicable, and feasible ideas. It can readily be understood that a project that involves many people, a great deal of machinery, and a substantial amount of financing, cannot afford the risk of too much experiment. As far as I can see, one good reason for this is the fact that, even if everything and everybody involved favors change, there is still an unknown quantity. Can you guess what it is? The answer is *the book buyer.*

I believe that all of us, publishers, editors, and designers, should be dedicated constantly to raising the level of knowledge as well as of good taste. I believe it is an obligation even though we do not take an Hippocratic oath. The great majority of the reading public might be able, and, in fact, willing, to accept new concepts in learning and perhaps, even in format, but experience teaches us that an almost immediate, resentful resistance appears and can destroy the publisher's best intentions before they can be tested fully. I wish I had an answer to this problem but, frankly, I don't. If I did, I would not be a book designer but, probably, the sales director of a million-dollar concern.

I do not wish to create the impression that I am a contradictory, paradox-loving creature, but I think it is the nature of the mind and all things creative often to be in direct contradiction. Perhaps when we strike out for something very new, we would really have it equally old and familiar. I believe it is less a question of being old or new than of being good. I must confess that I can be as enthusiastic about a truly original solution to an esthetic problem as about something old, good, and familiar. A thing of beauty need not be new or old—it must make one want to be very still and hope for the spell to remain unbroken. Thus, we can live with the past and with the future, which link our fathers and our children.

The trend of book design is naturally changing all the time. It never quite crystallizes until seemingly a few years later. Then, of course, it is quite easily discernible.

An attempt to evaluate the products in this ever-changing stream is difficult indeed. One of the primary formal means are the proliferating number of book shows, major and minor. The ground rules in each show are different, and some tend to be rather rigid. Committees and juries are subjective in their approach to the problem of setting down a reliable measure of quality. Occasionally the jury supplies their opinions on which each selection is based. More often the show stands and is open to criticism (reasonable and unreasonable). Personally, I have found the Children's Book Shows **very** successful. They have been staged at irregular intervals and have taken into consideration books published over a period of two or more years.

Generally speaking, books singled out for the honor of a show should be well designed, printed, and bound. They should present an attractive "package" which includes or ought to include good materials, primarily, of course, the paper on which the book is printed. It is regrettable, but happens often, that even very well planned books lose out because of poor quality in presswork and/or binding. Although judgment of design is highly subjective, anyone can tell an attractive sheet from a grayish, spongy one. Most people can tell when a book is carelessly printed, particularly if there are illustrations. Everyone has seen sloppy stamping and paste or glue squeezed out of a book which could be neither opened nor closed successfully. It is rare indeed to find particularly outstanding stamping jobs, sharp and accurate, nor are the brass binders' dies often etched and finished as well as they could be. Some offset work as well as letterpress comes out uneven and spoils the overall effect.

Of course, frequently, even the best planned typography goes sour, either because there has been a long lapse of time between the conception of the design and the final execution, or simply because of some interfering element or another.

As it is rare that all elements of the book's production will be of equally superior quality we must be satisfied to find a limited number of books which say eloquently that everybody concerned with them "cared." Conservative or modern design doesn't enter here as we are concerned with the overall effect, and it is just not possible to ram modernism down the throats of those who have grown up in the publishing world of yesterday. The modern designer who can combine his talent with the spirit of the present and with the tradition of book-making and cope with the miscellaneous technical handicaps and restrictions will be heard, and will be appreciated. Just to be different for the sake of being different strikes me as being on a par with pop artists who indeed are different, as were the paint sprinklers and geometrists. Remember you don't only want to *look* at a book, you also want to read it *and* enjoy it. I find interpretation of a manuscript by a designer to *his* advantage unfair to the author and to the reader.

It is true that the basic idea of the various shows is to encourage quality in book-making and I believe if we were to assemble in one place all the books that have been selected through the last thirty years or so we would have a splendid cross-section of American book-making of the last three or four decades. Of course, many would be missing, and others would not have much merit.

If we could indeed sponsor, arrange, and make a reality a truly representative show of American book-making I would like to see *all* categories under one roof and I would include book jackets if only to encourage those who feel as I do that jacket and format should have unity and continuity.

The American Institute of Graphic Arts was established in 1914. Its aim was and still is, broadly, the promotion of graphic arts in America. In a recent statement, the AIGA has this to say about itself: "It is the oldest and largest organization in the United States devoted to the interests of the creators and users of all the graphic arts—businessmen of many specialties, artists, craftsmen. Craftsmen all, in the products of print: Books in all categories—adult, juvenile, textbook and paperbound; direct and space advertisements; printed sales promotion materials; record album covers; packages and labels; periodicals." The AIGA, a nonprofit institution, provides "a meeting place for the exchange of ideas; a continuing series of exhibits, both in the United States and abroad, designed to record and encourage progress in the graphic arts; analytical seminar discussions devoted to the improvement of quality . . . a unique workshop in hand typesetting and printing design."

It was a wise decision by the AIGA to establish a yearly selection of well-designed and well-printed books, the Fifty Books of the Year. Later, the Institute expanded its activities well beyond the Fifty Books—with regular textbook, children's book and paperback shows, and with competitions and exhibits in many other fields of graphics. But all the same, the Fifty Books has remained a great event for the AIGA.

Like any great institution, the show has been open as much to criticism as to praise. There has been much disagreement among the members on the purpose and on how to run Fifty Books.

I don't know why fifty was chosen as an adequate number, but it serves the purpose very well. Since the books are supposed to be excellent in every physical respect, it would be quite a task for an average viewer to examine and appreciate a larger number than fifty. This is particularly true since the show has been sent traveling to many cities and university centers in the United States and Europe.

It is not surprising to me when people not in the book industry, and for that matter, some who are, refer to the Fifty Books of the Year as the "Fifty Best Books."

The urge to label things "Better" "Best" "Great" "Greatest" and regrettably, too, "Most Valuable" is the same as getting awards for accomplishing "More" than the next man. Thus new films are praised in trite superlatives. Whenever the Madison Avenue Boys toot their tinny blaring trumpets we are supposed to listen attentively, be awed or stunned by the "message from the sponsor," and most of all not to delay the purchase of the "great product."

To me it is immensely gratifying to see that our

concert halls and opera houses don't—at least not yet—embellish the names of composers and their works in this manner. Nor do the museums, nor the libraries. Why then the Fifty "Best" Books?

The function of the Fifty Books of the Year, as clearly and annually stated by the AIGA, is to single out fifty books which in the opinion of a small jury (usually three people) are designed with excellence, composed well, printed beautifully on good paper, and bound carefully. There are no rules to say what constitutes excellent design. The jurors must use their own judgment. No consideration is given to the jacket or to the literary content of the book. It is noteworthy that in the last forty-four years, in which 2,200 books have been chosen, practically all styles of book design, from the very traditional to the most experimental, have been included.

If a larger group of jurors than three were to undertake the judging of the hundreds of books annually entered for the Fifty, it would take them months instead of weeks to make choices, and there would be even more disagreement than there is now.

Often, jurors are themselves designers, and while they are modest enough not to select their own books, the other judges often do. This may seem odd to the public, but usually it would be poor judgment to omit those books. I know of one case in which a judge had not entered any of his own books, and the other judges went out to a bookstore and purchased some of his titles to include in the show.

The idea of breaking up the "Fifties" into several categories has often been discussed but has not really found enough support. So it may come to pass that one year we have more expensive art books, another year more University Press books, and sometimes a spate of "Promotion Books."

The quantity of books that we print and bind makes it not impossible but unlikely for us to produce more than a very small percentage of beautiful books.

There have been years when the judges could not find fifty books which they thought worthy of inclusion, and some years there were so many fine books that some had to be excluded, much to the judges' regret. However, it is quite obvious that the books selected were often not average trade books, but expensive art books, university press quality books, and various other books on which attention to detail has been lavished. Consequently, the average effort is overlooked and those who are involved in the making of such books are not particularly encouraged to extend themselves.

Some years ago I saw an exhibit at the Museum of Modern Art in New York. It was called "Useful Articles Priced Below $10." At least that might have been the title of the exhibit. Each article, many of them made for use in the household, carried such information as its price and where it could be found and purchased. The exhibits were all examples of fine design without regard to price. It has often occurred to me and probably to others in the book industry that there should be more exhibits of books not limited to peak accomplishments, but proving that improvements in format and production are constantly taking place. At the same time such shows could stimulate book sales in general.

A word to publishers: To enter a great many undistinguished books in the Fifty Books on the theory that one or another may score is to waste your money and the judges' time. The time to think of having your books included in the Fifty Books is when you get them designed and produced, not when you enter them just before the deadline. A stunning design sometimes pulls up mediocre production but the reverse is not usually true. The truth is that there are good materials available in abundance and many of them not uneconomical, that good composition, good pen work and good binding are by no means as hard to find as one might think. To combine excellence in planning the format, choosing the materials and arranging the production is the secret.

Concerning Frankfurt am Main, some facts are well-known—for instance, that it was a town where German emperors were crowned; that Goethe lived there; that it is a trade center; and that it is the place where the international book world meets annually for the Frankfurt Book Fair. But I doubt that many of our book people have visited the *Stiftung Buch-kunst*, the Book Art Foundation.

Physically, the foundation consists of a few large rooms primarily used for exhibits or lectures. In addition, there is a fine library and office. It is situated in an attractive residential part of Frankfurt, taking up the space of two apartments in a small house.

It is run by Dr. Georg Kurt Schauer, and what better man could there be for such a post? Dr. Schauer, who for years was production manager for the large and distinguished book publishing house of S. Fischer in Berlin, and later on a publisher of fine books himself, knows as much of books as anyone I have ever met.

He is, as is fitting, a scholar and artist. His knowledge is not limited to the history of printing, to book-making, and to book materials. He is a literary man in the best sense of the word. He knows type and type designers as well as printers and bookbinders. He has helped young designers and illustrators. In short, he is an ideal man for the job.

What is this job? Perhaps it would be best to explain first the components of such a foundation and then familiarize ourselves with those supporting it.

To start with, there is the library. It consists not only of those books selected by various juries throughout the last decades as "the most beautiful books of the year" (in contrast to our Fifty Books, the German selection is not bound to any arbitrary figure), but also of additional books considered worthy of inclusion in such a library by Dr. Schauer. There is, of course, the usual material on paper, type-setting, and printing.

From time to time exhibits are arranged showing the work of designers or illustrators, or perhaps of new typefaces.

The showcases themselves are beautiful to behold and add to the attractiveness of the material dis-played in them. Needless to say, a thorough job of writing, printing, and displaying of captions is done. With the exhibitions, catalogs are created that are collector's items in themselves. When no specific exhibition is planned, there is always enough material available for semipermanent exhibits to bridge the gap.

The foundation's library is a place of quiet dignity in which scholars do research, and in this silence a young designer may learn a great deal. The office, however, is always busy.

Established in 1964 by Dr. Schauer, the foundation is supported equally by groups in the German book industry—those whose sincere interest in beautiful books takes expression in the publishing, printing and binding, and selling of books. Among other supporting groups is the paper industry. Its backing is significant because of the special relationship between the European book and paper industries. Books published in Europe come in many sizes and are printed on an astounding variety of sheets. Apparently, the paper mills are willing and able to make very large varieties in small quantities. This means, of course, that they must be able at short notice to make added quantities of any given size to meet demands for unexpected additional printings.

Large, powerful and financially potent organizations of publishers, manufacturers, and booksellers have been supporting the foundation consistently. The burden of support is not heavy for any one group, and the collective effort offers much to the industry as a whole.

The publishers can see, at the foundation, how the book arts are practiced throughout the publishing world. The paper and cloth manufacturers can show samples of their merchandise in the finest possible setting. Printers and bookbinders can point with pride to the books they have helped to manufacture. Money is a very small price to pay for the articulate beauty and organized showing of their combined outputs.

Perhaps in being close to the fairly permanent beautiful artifacts of our time, almost anyone can appreciate how much love goes into the making of books. This is very clear to those who love books, but probably surprising to those for whom the writing, publishing, and selling of a book means merely dollars and cents.

In my professional career I have made many friends and, I suppose, some enemies. I have worked with many people—with some regularly, with others occasionally—and I have learned from practically everyone. Among the many there have been four in particular to whom I owe a debt of gratitude for friendship and kindness, wisdom and guidance.

MAURICE S. KAPLAN

Maurice S. Kaplan (1908-1951) was a book designer. I met him briefly at the Composing Room, where he had a studio, and then when he designed for Henry Holt & Company, before he went free lance in 1948. It was during the Holt period that we became friends, and we remained friends until he died of a heart attack. Maury was an ideal designer. He had started out with his own little print shop in Detroit before he came to New York to work for book publishers. His deep intellectual interest made him particularly valuable to his employers, especially when he became a free lancer. It was wonderful to see him work, for he had a flair for book design and was neither ponderous nor careless. It was one of his very good habits to make copies of all of his layouts before he sent them to the publisher. We used to meet regularly once a week for lunch, if possible, and talk about our work and customers. We truly shared our knowledge, and agreed, without any formality, not to touch each other's accounts. This is particularly noteworthy, as each of us was occasionally approached by a publisher for whom the other was working and we turned these approaches aside. I don't know of any similar arrangements, but I do know of the opposite.

I think, primarily, I learned from Maury not to feel too important. His wonderful sense of humor gave me some lightness, too. Never have I before or after found anyone who was so willing to help at a moment's notice. Wherever he went, his warm and gay manner brought him friends.

I remember that very shortly after his death a few of us in the industry met to discuss setting up a scholarship in his name, and when I was stumped in drawing up some specifications, I found myself automatically picking up the telephone to dial his number. This time he was not there to give me advice.

KURT WOLFF

Kurt Wolff (1886-1963) was one of the rare publishers of our time who published only books he believed in. His first publishing venture was established in Munich, Germany, in 1908. His firm published the works of some of the most outstanding German and American writers. Kurt Wolff and his wife, Helen, established a new publishing house, Pantheon Books, in New York in 1941. Its first office was a part of the Wolff's studio apartment on Washington Square. Physically, the firm never became big, but every book he ever published was individually discovered, obtained, or created. To use a term from music, the books were produced *con amore*. The love for good books or fine books alike, and best of all, from my point of view, for good *and* good-looking books, was second nature to Kurt Wolff. He might easily have been a successful designer had he not preferred to be a publisher. In his dealings with book manufacturers he was friendly and understanding, which 20 odd years ago was rather the exception.

It was at that time that I realized that I did not have to work *for* anyone, but that I could work *with* customers. There is no doubt that Kurt Wolff influenced my ways of thinking and designing, and greatly stimulated me intellectually. Traditional as he was, with the humanistic knowledge that a fine education had given him, he also had the executive's talent for getting the best out of his co-workers. This was instinctive with him and not artificial; and he avoided anything too "big," any superorganization or super-project. His was a real charm, that of heart and intellect united.

WILLIAM P. GLEASON

William P. Gleason (1915-1965) was basically a salesman. After an apprenticeship with William Rudge, fine printers of New York, he became associated with the Colonial Press of Clinton, Massachusetts, and developed its New York office. For a time, Colonial and "Bill" Gleason became synonymous. A few years ago he left Colonial to join the Lindenmeyr Paper Company, paper merchants to the book industry. Bill was very well known in the publishing industry and a much sought-for helper and organizer in all printing activities. Like Maury Kaplan, he could set type and run a press. I have rarely known a salesman who knew equipment better and had more patience with the customers. Sometimes I used to watch him at his crowded desk, coping with frantic customers and uncooperative plant personnel, usually promoting an atmosphere of peace.

Working with Bill was almost like owning part of the plant, a gift which he couldn't very well make because he didn't own any part of it himself—either Colonial or Lindenmeyr. I doubt that there will be another Bill Gleason around so soon.

GORDON S. IERARDI

Gordon S. Ierardi (1917-1966) was my neighbor and friend for twenty years. We met mostly in our home community, dealing with his children and mine and with community activities such as book fairs. His whole career as a traveler and editor was with John Wiley & Sons. As is well known, "Gord" developed and maintained for Wiley one of the finest psychology departments in the country. When I think of him, as I do frequently, I think primarily of his unfailing integrity which made him an honest publisher and a fair friend.

It was, of course, a great deal of fun for me to be able to talk to him in his home or mine or on commuters' trains and to exchange thoughts on publishing and even production. I cannot emphasize enough the fact that anyone who is called "a publisher" must be versatile, articulate, and efficient as Gordon was. There have been many such men in the history of American book publishing, and I have been privileged to have had some friends among them.

In the course of the last thirty odd years, I have seen practically all the publishing offices in this country. One of the best ones I have ever known began in a one-room apartment on Washington Square South. The shipping room was a converted bathroom with most wrapping materials resting in the bathtub. I have seen more munificently equipped places, well carpeted offices with bookcases filled with books rarely touched by human hands, penthouses and the like, but recently I was privileged to see one of the very best, consisting in effect, of one large open office and only one comparatively private office for the manager. Everyone else was sitting at antiquated, overloaded desks. No one had more than a desk, a chair to sit on, a chair for a possible visitor, and a telephone. No carpeting, no bar, no conference table, no gold lettered names, no radios, no air of elegance.

Yet everyone I met on this day did his or her work with enthusiasm and dedication, with talent and knowledge, which as a combination can rarely be found anymore in our part of town. Conspicuously absent were sales, publicity, and advertising departments. There did not seem to be an atmosphere of how much money could be made or might be lost in any given year. All the same, several hundred new titles are being produced yearly, and several thousand are kept on the active list. This little office, which seems to contain hardly more than forty people gives you a feeling that more is at stake than a best seller or an adoption. New projects are in the air, and I have no doubt that five o'clock is not the end of all activity.

The books are not paperbacks or hardcover editions; they are "talking books" (recorded books in 16 rpm), tapes, and books in Braille. The place is the Division for the Blind, Library of Congress, Washington, D.C.

UV

Part Six: Travels and Thoughts

W

I have always

been interested in materials for which I had no immediate use or need, such as quantities of pencils, papers, or even molds for picture frames.

I have used one very attractive mold to make a quantity of frames for old manuscript pages, interesting end papers, old woodcuts and engravings.

I wished to have a few maps framed. Calling a local frame maker, I said foolishly, perhaps, "How much will it cost to make four picture frames 20 x 16 inches?" The frame maker replied that he could not give me such an estimate. I added hastily, "What I mean is, how much would you charge to mat four maps, supply the glass, cut the molds, and finish the frames?" The voice on the other end of the telephone said in a surly manner, "How should I know what kind of molds you want? The price will depend on that." I informed him that I had the mold. His answer came back "You hava the molds, you maka the frames!"

This year's crop of Christmas cards (150 sent out, 120 received) showed—in our opinion—a further marked decrease in taste. There were, of course, numerous, most conventional types of cards; snow and sleighs and red, green and gold glitter abounded. Imprints were invariably vermillion. Some tall cards were solid gold and stamped, raised or embossed— else the type belonged to a minor species of script faces.

Of course, there were some cards in good taste. But they were few. If any change could be noted, it was the switch from museum cards to the solid gold, heavily embossed.

It may come as a surprise to my friends and readers that I own, administer, and daily visit a museum. True, it is only two feet by four feet in size, consisting of fifteen cubicles of dark wood against a translucent glass wall, and it currently houses no more than fifty items such as eighteenth century decorated bottles, steins and various articles of the same period made of pewter, brass, copper, or painted wood.

Their value to me is their beauty and the story they tell. Occasionally I change the exhibits, but never much as I don't seem to tire of them. I call it "the museum" and admission is always free.

The western world has many great museums. Some house art, some artifacts, some are dedicated to the many facets of science. There are enormous museums, middle sizes ones and also rather small but precious exhibits. Many libraries could easily be museums as well.

It is obvious that we have learned a good deal about what a museum can do for its visitors. We know about optimum sizes of its buildings, of the lighting, the arrangement, and flexibility of the exhibits. We feel we know what the average visitor expects to find and how much he can absorb without mental (or physical) fatigue or boredom.

Some of the famous museums are exceedingly large because it takes so much space to house their collections (or accumulations) which are ever growing through acquisitions or bequests. As trends in art appreciation have changed, large numbers of (often large) paintings are removed from the walls merely to be carefully put away in the museum's storage rooms. Or else a museum might have too many works of one artist or may discover unhappily that paintings attributed to a great master are copies or works by his pupils.

On the other side, smaller towns or colleges wish to improve the quality and quantity of a local "Historical Society." Naturally it takes enormous funds to stock even a smaller building with the "great masters."

Sometimes museums feature one great painter of local origin and turn over part of the building to changing exhibits. There is a museum in Oslo which has a great collection of the Norwegian impressionist painter, Munch. The Municipal Museum in Amsterdam has a very large number of the finest van Goghs, and the Municipal Museum in Basel shows paintings and the very interesting sketches for which Hans Holbein is famed.

The museum I would like to describe here is the Gutenberg Museum in Mainz, Germany. It is an entirely new building which opened its doors to the public two or three years ago. A rather compact building in the middle of a garden, it consists of four stories and a basement. Each floor has two levels, which I find a very refreshing departure from the standard enormous floors. The levels are just a few steps above and below each other. In the center of the building there are stairs and an elevator.

On one of the floors a Gutenberg Bible is housed in a fireproof walk-in vault. It seems better protected than other Gutenberg Bibles I have seen at the Morgan and Huntington Libraries or at Yale and at the New York Public Library, but an expert on safes told me that the immense heat created by a major fire would cause any paper or vellum inside of the seemingly well-protected vault to char.

To appreciate what this museum has to offer, one begins in modern museum fashion at the top floor where a replica of Gutenberg's first shop is on display. As the museum owns some of the original matrices from which type can be cast, a sheet of two handset pages of the 42-line Bible is printed right on the same kind of press as the one used by Gutenberg. The paper approximates paper mouldmade in those times.

Throughout the Museum there are shown the slow but steady developments in machinery—presses up to a present day Heidelberg two-color vertical, and typesetting equipment such as Monotypes and Linotypes since 1886.

In addition, as well as one of the original copies of the Gutenberg Bible, there are numerous examples of fine book printing during the last 500 years. Many countries are represented. Exhibits change frequently but indicate that the art of printing books is not dead.

This museum quite naturally contains many rare books, which made me feel that the rare book departments of colleges abounding in wonderful material could bring them even closer to the student body and the townspeople if some space were devoted to such technical exhibits as paper, type, and some printing equipment, much in the manner of the Gutenberg Museum.

When a museum or a library is merely large it may seem dead to those who have not somehow been stimulated previously by the arts. The Gutenberg Museum in Mainz, teeming with people that day, proved conclusively to me that people will be interested in art if it is made palatable and accessible to them.

Of two tourists of the same background who went through Europe for more than two months last summer, one was enthusiastic about the close to twenty museums she visited and enjoyed, and the other informed me she had planned to go to a big museum but did not like the building and never bothered to look at its inside.

It seems a coincidence that in five hundred years of printing two of the finest examples of printing—and there have been many—came from that little German town and from an even smaller place in New England. It may even be a coincidence that both books are bibles printed *ad majorem gloriam dei*, but I don't think so.

What has fascinated me, and surely many others who love books and the art of printing, is the complete and utterly artless conception of these two— the Gutenberg Bible and the Bruce Rogers Bible.

I have read many books, looked at many more. I have designed some but never have I forgotten the thrilling moment when I first pulled a sheet of paper from the only too-generously inked type I had been able to compose with the meager supply of type in my first toy printing set. I tried again—it worked again and again. Did I misspell, set type upside down or anything else requiring correction? I don't know, I cannot remember. All I know is that I ran to show my work to my mother.

Do we really know what Gutenberg may have felt when his first sheet "came off press"? Whether he knew, imagined, dreamed of what his invention would do for and to the world? He must have worked hard to perfect a type face that could pass for the handiwork of an accomplished scribe. He had to design an alphabet, many abbreviations or ligatures, capital letters and small initials. The large initials were undoubtedly planned to be left to the great skill of the finest scribes and in fact to the painters of the period, some famous but preferring to remain anonymous in this industrial occupation.

I want to say here that no matter what the value of a Gutenberg Bible—and there are other more valuable books—I have never seen better book design, type design, page layout and presswork. I have also seen many beautiful manuscripts, but nothing has ever thrilled me more than this great work of art.

During the next five hundred years, many printers in many lands invented better presses, designed new typefaces, many of great beauty. There were, of course, fashions and trends, experiments, new concepts of typography—but some basic facts remained. Facts such as the proportion of a book page, the printing in clear black ink on good white paper, the traditional harmony of centric design. It became and remained apparent to many of us, that tricky design might please a designer, perhaps a publisher, but not often a reader.

It was in this vein that a great printer of this century executed a commission for the Oxford University Press of England (itself almost as old as the art of printing) to design and supervise the printing of a bible. This bible, usually known by the name of its designer, Bruce Rogers, is now a showpiece of printing in the twentieth century and perhaps destined to survive as long in history as the 42-line bible by Johannes Gutenberg.

It is of exquisite beauty, set in a bold, direct, deceivingly simple manner in Bruce Rogers' Centaur type. The harmony between the title page, the chapter openings (Books of the Old and New Testaments) and the text pages is complete.

I would not like the reader to think that all I appreciate or admire in printing are these two books. That is not so. There are many that I know, some that I own, which are beautiful, worth the eternal life a good book should lead. But these two are surely the finest I know.

Museums can be amazingly rewarding but also disappointing. An hour in an unheated, old, dark building can be just that when there seems to be nothing but Gothic stone sculptures—but wait—here is something. It turns out to be a printed page in a frame about 8½" x 11".

This little item with no identification whatsoever held my attention one very cold day in the fall a few years ago. The place was the Municipal Museum in Lübeck, Germany. This town, known as a "Free Hause City" in the middle ages, equal then in importance as a trading post to London, Antwerp, Hamburg and Copenhagen, has more recently acquired fame for its sweet Marzipan and its bitter "Death Strip" which goes right through the town, separating it from East Germany.

The "Death Strip" is a strip of land 200 to 300 feet wide, which runs from the Baltic Sea to Czechoslovakia, has on it no buildings, trees or even grass. It is ploughed and prepared in such a manner that no one can cross it without being noticed by the East German border guards. While it is rarely crossed from the west, or even approached without apprehension, persons from the east seeking to cross risk being shot.

Well, to come back to the Museum, it was Friday afternoon. A telephone call the next day yielded only the scanty information that the curator would be on hand the next Monday and no one else knew anything about the little page. I could not wait.

Soon I was back at home and after a while the memory of the page haunted me. The fact is that I felt I was hot on the trail of a great typographical discovery. The more I thought about the page, which I had by this time identified as a Missal page, it looked to me like one of Gutenberg's type faces. It was printed with a beautiful, sharp impression with black and red ink on vellum, but as soon as I looked at specimens of the Gutenberg Bible I knew it was not the same type. Even my elementary knowledge told me that certain caps (there were very few on the page) and one or two of the "lower case" letters were different. Not much, to be sure, but some.

First I went to the rare book division in the New York Public Library to compare the little photograph I finally obtained from Lübeck (it took ten weeks of correspondence). A visit to the Morgan Library yielded even more discoveries. By now I had learned to identify type of the period of the "Incunabula" (printing in the 15th Century since its inception, literally "cradle printing"). This was no small undertaking. There were several hundred alphabets to be compared with my little sample. If one considers the caps, lower case letters and the many additional abbreviations then in use, the task was formidable, requiring time and good eyes.

I was willing and I remember that when I left the Morgan Library after six hours of intensive application of all I knew—dog-tired, hungry and happy—I had found what I was looking for.

In fact, I had found more than that. When I had settled down comfortably and very peacefully with two very large volumes in front of me, a little white pad, a pencil, and my sample, I could not anticipate how far the alphabetical journey of early printers would carry me. The letter K yielded the first and, I

thought, only clue. Konrad Kachelofen of Nuremberg clearly used the typeface that I had admired so
much for the last half year. Everything checked. As I
only had one page and the old alphabets are usually
identified by the shape of the cap M—which my
page did not contain—I had to fall back on other
letters, quite a few of them. Still, Kachelofen (tile
stove) was my man.

In my first flush of excitement, and, I thought,
luck, I continued to scan the following pages for a
similar alphabet to make sure. Alas, very soon my
efforts were crowned by more success than I had
bargained for. It seemed that a printer by the name
of Lotter had what I felt was the identical type face,
and he had printed a Missal or two. But he lived in
Leipzig. This town, situated in Saxony, was and is a
few hundred miles from Nuremberg, then a prosper-
ous guild town in Bavaria.

There were messengers on horseback taking letters even then—five hundred years ago. I don't know
about mail coaches in that era; but whatever mode of
transportation was used, how did they transport
hundreds of pounds of type? Or did they? Whose
type was designed, punched, and cast first? Who sold
to whom, or were the punches perhaps stolen by
some medieval thief?

All this went through my head as I compared the
alphabets of the two master printers. At last a horrible thought struck me. Could there be three, or

more? What had been pleasure now became a difficult task and almost an obsession. Two hours later, I had ploughed through the entire alphabet of alphabets. I did discover one more printer, Georg Stuchs, also in Leipzig. I felt relieved that he did not work in a third city, and I began to believe that the Nuremberger probably maintained a mail order business, or its equivalent, in type and what not.

However, I was exhausted and not a little pleased and I decided to call it a day. When I left the library I realized I had spent an entire day without doing my work or calling customers. I had not even thought of calling anyone on the telephone.

One answer to my triangular problem I got from a bibliography on that period. Mr. Stuchs was simply the son of Mr. Lotter, or vice versa. Perhaps he had been an apprentice in the Nuremberg shop, then journeyed from town to town on foot as was customary with "journeymen" of the period, obtained employment in Leipzig and then finally married the master's daughter.

I still do not know how the type made its way across Germany. To be sure, they did not have a "Death Strip" then. But there were highwaymen, and I suspect they were no more interested in type at that time than a similar character today would be in books—but they did have Marzipan even then. The Crusaders brought it across the Mediterranean from the Holy Land.

At the occasion of the Fifty Books Dinner, the great yearly event of the American Institute of Graphic Arts, a warm, very friendly note was introduced by the main speaker, Frederick Adams, Jr. of the Morgan Library. He noted the interest the library was taking in producing all printed matter and for that matter, lettered signs, etc., as well as possible, done by the best craftsmen in the field. It is granted that they can afford it. But it was obvious that a good deal of care is given here—as well as planning by the client himself. I gather that there are fewer crises, emergencies, and catastrophes. An institution owning *two* Gutenberg Bibles and untold treasures, from the earliest scrolls and manuscripts to some of the newest and finest printed books could be expected to be *very* fussy about its ephemera but actually they are more understanding than some people at one historical restoration project.

I hear that there a book is a book only if sewn on a hand binder's frame and bound in leather. Bad news for commercial bookbinders! Much as I love these books in my library and for that matter in anybody's library that fall in the former category, I am most willing to accept the latter if their contents warrants my reading them and preferably if they are designed well and printed well on good (good-looking) paper. Let history take care of which books survive. Every now and then you can buy leather-bound tomes properly sewn on bands at a sale conducted

usually by the book department of a quality department store. They give your home class but I doubt
anyone ever reads them.

"Battery-powered lanterns are available to the public." This friendly bit of information comes from a
small folder of the Isabella Stewart Gardner Museum
in Boston, more often called "Mrs. Gardner's" or, by
the proper Bostonians, "Mrs. Jack Gardner's." This
lovely, small private museum situated around the
corner from the Fine Arts Museum has changed little
since Mrs. Gardner's death more than half a century
ago. You can still see some velvet draped under a
painting with a vase of flowers just as it was during
the lifetime of Mrs. Gardner. Hence, "battery-powered lanterns," more commonly known as flashlights.

In the course of a short vacation this past summer, I
had occasion to visit two fine paper mills. As a pre-
text for engaging in this activity, I had suggested to
my wife that life is incomplete without a visit to a
major paper mill. For bait, I dangled the prospect of
plenty of fresh lobsters, fresh from the sea to pound
to plate, and, a handful of miles west of the sea, the
glory of great music at Tanglewood! It worked!
    Our first stop was Portland, not far from the
Maine Turnpike. The unmistakable aroma directed
us better than the signs. It was worth the smell,
though. It is forever fascinating to see and hear the

big four-foot logs crashing into the enormous metal drums, to be chewed by the rotating knives into small chips. Pressure-cooking here is not an emergency measure half an hour before dinner, but an operation that cooks tons of wood chips with chemicals as the first important step toward the raw material called pulp. A further group of operations finally produces a white substance looking like a cross between wet blotting paper and pot cheese. Eventually this mush is mixed with ninety-nine parts water to each part of pulp and is off at a fast clip on the way to becoming one fresh, endless stream of paper. On this trip of only a few hundred feet, taking a fraction of a minute, ninety-five parts of water are shed, leaving the end product containing 4 percent of moisture, needed to keep the paper from being brittle. The paper is trimmed on both sides, miraculously by a jet stream of water, passed between many heated rollers, traveling on a wire mesh on felt losing water all the time. All the while, the fibers are being straightened to lie in the machine direction.

It is no secret that the paper mills in this country are running seven days a week around the clock. We learned a few new facts, new to me that is, such as the use of hardwood as well as needle trees.

One week and many lobsters later, we stopped at another mill, this one specializing in 100 percent rag papers, stationery, and bank notes, generally. Instead of the crashing logs, there were soft smooth cotton cuttings—presumably there are no more rag pickers! For the banknote paper, 50 percent flax is used, the raw material for linen. A different odor filled the air, less chemical but still unmistakably that of paper-making. Mentioning that we had previously visited a big mill in Maine, brought the rather unexpected response that they probably made newsstock or tissues. We denied this, indignantly, knowing better. After all, how many letters do we write and how few sheets of bank notes pass through our hands, compared with the books we read and design! We refrained from further visits to paper mills during the vacation and concentrated on music, quiet relaxation, and planning for the next trip, when and if.

During the month of October each year, as the leaves around the cities become colorful and find their way into the gutters of suburban houses, it becomes time to look forward to the annual picnic at "Sybil's Cave." Will there be rain or sunshine? The place is near Tarrytown, New York, and is situated in an abandoned quarry overgrown now with plant life. Some of the attractive little houses in Tarrytown were built with the stone quarried here. This comment, however, is not an architectural exercise, but a belated recognition of a beautiful day of fellowship among people who, for a Saturday afternoon, have come away from their printing orders and telephones.

For many years Sybil Hastings, the lady who put

color into *Columbia* Mills, has been the gracious hostess of this picnic.

As at a New Year's Eve party, people come and go, although the invitation reads, "From noon to sundown," and I suspect that sometime there have been gay stragglers into the wee hours of the morning.

Cars arrive from at least three states and park between trees or occasionally, after a solid day of rain in Westchester, deep in mud. A long table is set out, dominated by a businesslike bar which is presided over by Harry U. Hayes. On the other tables, usual and unusual foods are prepared in barbecue fashion, but the perennial favorites continue to be tiny cocktail frankfurters called Smokies (best frankfurters this side of the Atlantic) and tiny fried chicken legs partially wrapped in aluminum foil.

It is an unbelievably colorful crowd. Old-timers mingle with kids hardly more than a few months in the book industry and at any moment ready to break out into guitar playing and sad, sad songs. There are production managers and manageresses, designers, accountants, editors, wives, husbands, and children.

It is a time and place for old friendships and new, a time not to be formal ("come in old clothes"), a time to talk shop but not business, and a time to drink with Bob Harper, president of Columbia Mills, who will photograph you when you least expect it, a time to visit with gracious Jim and Mickie Reynolds and other Syracusans, and mostly a time to have fun.

Why does a modest lodge in New England often have a larger library than a luxury resort hotel? Could it be that the luxury tourists enjoying the swimming pool and three enormous meals a day don't read? I have stayed at the two best hotels in Mallorca, Spain and I can count on my fingers the times I have seen people with a book (opened or closed) in their hands.

I have made a private little study of how many books (paperback) are sold in the inevitable little souvenir shoppes. Handbags, pearls, scarves, *si*, books, *no!* On the other hand, of course, magazines abound. I don't even care to describe them, as they depend almost entirely on sensationalism; the French, German, Italian, etc, are all culpable.

I have, however, spent many enjoyable hours with a transistor radio, listening to the oh so British comments on Kenya, swim meets, Scottish holidays and "crofts" which the BBC (British Broadcasting Corporation) tirelessly supplies. I have listened to Paris, Stockholm, Holland and to the many Soviet-run stations in Moscow, Berlin, Budapest, Bucharest, Sofia, etc. For my benefit (I take it) they are sent in English and more often in German—although it is a quaint, hard-bitten kind quite different from that of West Germany. These stations discuss such topics as the merits of Iron Curtain science, even agriculture (for the benefit of Africa), news about Viet Nam and sometimes send classical music. They never advertise anything but Communism—it is always called "democratic." Paris will advertise *la cigarette Ariel, mentholisee,* and Mallorca interrupts operas, concerts and just Flamenco with enthusiastic offers of pearls, mode haute couture, and travel ideas. This shows how the Western countries have become Americanized, except for the BBC.

A visit to a local printer and to a bookbinder yielded little of interest, There are no quaint, old presses, no wonderful "handbound" books. The quality leaves a great deal to be desired, at least by our standards and those of the continent. I have heard of interesting places in "Argelia," more specifically, in "Argel," which is Algiers, but I am not going to chance disappearance in the Casbah just to please my readers. Incidentally, I should have mentioned that there are many Arabic radio stations and it *is* interesting to hear their music. It is at once reminiscent of the staccato Spanish melodies of the Flamenco. It also reminds one of the wailing, drawn-out notes of near-Eastern or Jewish music.

One bit of wisdom that I, naturally, forget from trip to trip is to prepare carefully for it. There are three elements against the traveller who has definite ideas about what he wants to do or see. First, when you find yourself in any strange or foreign town, time is running out on you fast and expensively while you search for a good printer, for instance, who probably exists but whom no one knows. This is even more true when your only source for information is a willing but uninformed concierge in your hotel. He doesn't, couldn't know the difference between a large printer, a small printer and a fine printer (or binder). In a major town you may find a publisher who could tell you—if his office is not closed during July (often the case in Europe). The second element is the fact that such places as print shops and binderies may not be—in fact, naturally are not—on the main street of town. While it is likely that there are organizations that could help you hunt down your quarry, you have no idea what *their* names are. Finally, one can't tell without some expert briefing—if such is available—whether it is more profitable to see a large industrial graphic enterprise in or near town, or a magnificent hand binder in some distant little town or village. Again, my apologies, but I think the travelers may profit by my disappointment and prepare themselves in time for their trips.

Of course, you may see specimens of fine work *somewhere* and then hunt down the producer but I have not had that luck in Spain—so I have had to concentrate on the magnificent weather and on the playas (beaches) and what they have to offer.

This is written at the edge of a big reservoir that serves several big cities of a New England state. I have just heard some fantastic stories about strafing planes and target practice at this idyllic spot. I have seen a big beaver dam and enough wood cut down by the beavers to make paper for a bookstore full of paperbacks.

Last night I attended an auction in a small country town that yielded interesting information. The auctioneer, who was fast, amusing, and pleasant, auctioned off everything, obviously from the estate of an old, dying out family, in short order. Old kitchen equipment, kid gloves, toys, unmatched glassware, and china followed in rapid succession. I clocked him getting rid of twenty lots in five minutes. The lots went mostly at fifty cents or at one dollar each. After a short lull, he sold books from the library of the estate in lots of about twenty books each. Sets and little stacks of paperbacks followed. The audience just would not bid anything, even fifty cents, for the hardcover books, admittedly of the 1910-1920 variety, until he put up lots of about forty books which then sold for fifty cents a lot. The paperbacks, however, went very quickly in lots of twelve to fifteen at $1.00 to $1.50, depending on the contents, and I believe the buyers knew the titles very well. Hurrah for paperbacks!

XY

Part Seven: Notes to a Beginner

Z

Dear Miss X . . .

Received your package with various illustrations. . . . The following thoughts come to me more or less at random in regard to your problem as a free-lance illustrator living far away from the activity of the publishing houses in New York.

First of all, consider that you have a service to sell. Unless you are a famous artist, it is little use to go into a publishing house and simply say, "I have an idea for illustrating *The Emperor's New Clothes*" or "I have finished six or eight or ten full color paintings for this book." The publisher will probably explain to you, more or less patiently, that he really is not thinking of doing an illustrated edition of *The Emperor's New Clothes*, or, for that matter, any edition at all.

The way to go about selling your service, instead, is this:

1. Study the market. Who is in the business to put out children's books? If you are particularly interested in fairy tales or legends, who has been publishing such books recently?

2. Look at the books available to you and examine the style and method of illustration in which they have been done. Go to the largest library you can, and spend days and days looking at the new and old illustrated books. You will find many that are very beautifully illustrated. Look, for example, at the work of Arthur Rackham, who worked in London and who caught the spirit of fairy tale and legend admirably in his illustrations for the Ring of the Nibelung, Peter Pan and many fairy tales. Most of his works were water color paintings which were reproduced in the standard manner of four-color process and letterpress.

You mention the extensive four-color illustrations in a large publisher's series of books. What you don't realize is that such an organization with immense advertising capabilities, can afford a vast amount of color work because these books will be printed and sold in quantities of well over 100,000 copies or more. The publisher's cost of illustrations and reproduction is part of a formula. In contrast, if you were successful in selling some publisher the idea of putting out a new edition of a fairy tale or a collection by Andersen, it is not likely that his edition would exceed 10,000 or 15,000, and more than two colors would not be feasible because of the expense.

Consider another point. Even if there were a market for four-color illustration—and this is not an era in which there is a great demand for paintings of any sort in books—you would have to know first what the publisher would care to have illustrated. Then you would have to find out the size of the contemplated book. Your very large illustrations would reduce, of course, but they might not reduce suitably for a given trim size. The proportion would have to be right for the page. You would have to find out how many colors the publisher could use, and finally, you would have to sit down with the publisher's production people and see whether some of the costly color separations could be done by you. I think you could do it if you were told how. It is not as difficult as it may seem.

Now as for your illustrations: Aside from the matter of size, I would suggest that in order for you to visualize the end result, do not use large poster boards —at least, not for the sketches—but good white paper in the size of a book which you, yourself, may like for its size and feel. There are many trim sizes, but, again, I would suggest you go into a library, look at the books you like, bring a little pile of the books you like best to your table, have paper, pencil, and ruler ready, and measure them. It will give you some interesting and very simple facts. You will find that among the many books you see, there are a few standard sizes which are frequently used. These sizes are dictated largely by the size of the presses used.

As to your drawings, I like the color work and I also like the style of the line drawings. I believe they will go very well together in a book. Normally, from an aesthetic point of view, I would prefer only color or only line. But inasmuch as the publisher must expect the buying public to want as much color as possible, and he cannot afford color throughout, he may compensate by adding some black-and-white line drawings to the small number of color pages.

One very important point is this: If you were to take one or two of your illustrations, and reduce them by photostat to perhaps a third or 40 percent of their size, which would be about the right size for a book page, you might find that the heads and faces were too small. This points up the fact that you should always start—even in your first sketches—with what is called "same size"—the size in which the book will be printed. Suppose you expect the book to be 6 x 9 inches, or an oblong, 9 x 6; simply use some 6 x 9 paper for your drawing. You may find this rather limiting, but this is the challenge of all work. Without limits it might produce art, but it would not fit into the framework of book production.

If you can, try to spend a few weeks in New York City going to the public library and to bookstores. Try to visit four or five of the leading children's book departments of publishing houses. One way to select the publisher you want to meet is to see whose books you especially like. . . .

With very best wishes,

Stefan Salter

"How does a designer differ from an illustrator?" Let me say that just as an architect builds a house, so does an interior decorator decorate its inside.

Many books are designed by designers, and even those which are carelessly turned over directly to the printer are designed in some fashion. But few books are illustrated.

In illustration there are two major divisions: The fine art illustrations, which are used in fiction or non-fiction, and the more or less creative illustrations made for specific use in the important textbook field. Here, of course, the illustrator shares the field with photographs, and while many textbooks are illustrated almost extravagantly, there are very few trade books that get such treatment; in the trade the publisher cannot usually afford it. Of course, most juveniles are illustrated, and there is always a demand for newer and better illustrators using perhaps a novel approach.

Occasionally a designer can illustrate, but that is rare. However, illustrators who can design exist in greater numbers, and in particular, children's book illustrators like to design their own books.

The easiest, cheapest, and best method of becoming acquainted with book illustration and book design is to look at books as much as possible, to get to know the typefaces used, the methods of printing employed, and the styles of illustration. Take an interest in what is published here and abroad in all phases of publishing. Any single day, to say nothing of a number of single days, in a library will yield treasures and will give you free and rapid instruction. After awhile you will know at a glance what publisher's book you are holding in your hands, and you may even become familiar with designers and type faces, the names of which can often be found either on the copyright page backing up the title page, or occasionally on the colophon page, which some publishers print at the very end of the book. Mention is made here of the type face used, the designer, the manufacturer, and perhaps even the name of the paper.

How do we become successful Book Designers? How is one successful at any work ones does? I think that it is to be happy with one's medium, that it is knowing it as well as its tools, and the people who practice it.

To start with, it is fair to assume that you must bring a native talent to your chosen trade.

Talent for book designing shows up in different ways. There are probably not too many book designers in the field who intended to become book designers in the first place, but they drifted into it from various occupations within and without the publishing field, from jobs in the printing industry and, of course, from the art schools. In general, I would like to believe that all of them have in common not only artistic talent and a casual interest in books and the art of making books, but a feeling for books which is, or almost is, love for them.

Book designers are expected to have a good and varied background. A prospective book designer must then acquire as much technical knowledge as possible. A background in commercial art is most useful, including some knowledge of typography and a sure hand in preparing mechanicals, as well the ability to do lettering and perhaps some illustrating. Apprentices from the craft of printing have learned many of the basic rules for making layouts and designing pages, rules which can be applied with few variations to the designing of books. Anything that you can learn about paper, composition, and presswork is going to be useful to you when you deal with books. Experience in any area of the graphic arts is valuable for book design.

Art students, of course, may be prepared for a career in book design in many ways. Much is included in their curriculum. Practically everything they learn will become useful in any graphic arts career.

After your college career you may want to enroll for graduate studies in one of the following schools. Six come to mind of equal, if different, quality. In alphabetical order they are: Carnegie Institute of Technology, Pittsburgh, Pa.; Cooper Union, Astor Place, New York City; Philadelphia Museum of Fine Arts—School of Design; Rhode Island School of Design, Providence; School of Visual Arts, East 23rd Street, New York City; and the Yale School of Art and Architecture, Chapel and York Streets, New Haven, Connecticut.

All of these schools give degrees. Their programs are intended for students who can show ability in graphic design. The schools teach graphic design, typography, book design, book illustration, lettering, photography, even printing and binding. Their teachers are usually professionals of first standing. As much as possible these schools teach not only theory but also the practical side of design. The schools also arrange for numerous field trips to plants so that their students become familiar with machinery and merchandise. Generally speaking, there is absolutely no limit to the background of knowledge that a book designer can and does use in his work. A wide general background provides an ability to deal successfully with the tremendous variety of books as they are written, designed, and produced. They may be as different as books on art, medicine, or cooking; they may be illustrated children's books or college textbooks. I can say truthfully that any knowledge that I may have acquired before or during my career as a book designer has helped me almost as much as my typographical and technical background.

Education is a great thing. There is little that you cannot learn today at a college or in a technical school.

No matter how much technical knowledge the young designer brings to his job, a great deal of it is usually theoretical. Only the combination of higher education along with "on the job" training can give the proficiency and experience that makes our performance a success.

Within the first year of working for a commercial firm after you have finished your studies you will really learn what work is expected of you and how you are expected to do it. Whether you remain in one position throughout your career or change jobs occasionally, you will gradually learn all you need to know.

From the day that you are faced for the first time with a manuscript you are expected to design, to the time when you stop designing books—if that should ever happen —you will never stop learning. You will learn from knowledgeable people like your fellow designers, from the production people who have a great deal of experience, and from the plant people who have detailed technical knowledge. They will teach you methods, routines, and the practical side of designing. You can also learn from people who don't seem to have design knowledge or even much taste, but they see book design from another angle and it is important that you understand their points of view which can be similar to that of the ultimate readers who usually pay little attention to book design.

You will know soon enough what layout or tracing paper you like best, nine by twelve rather than twelve by eighteen, for instance. You will get used to working with hard pencils and pica rulers, and you will know what the layouts will look like when they come back from the publisher and the printer.

You will become attached to book papers perhaps because of their textures and shades. In dealing with book cloth you may prefer the rough "linen finish" to a smooth buckram. You will have strong likes and dislikes for type faces. Perhaps type faces such as Weiss and Palatino will attract you, perhaps Times Roman and Optima. But only experience will teach you something about the religious and classical feeling of the former and the modern and technical feeling of the latter. There are no successful rules on what type fits what book. Your taste, your instinct, and your experience will be the best judges. You will also learn to compromise, using type faces not merely because they please you, but because they are available and, when used, will make the book run the proper number of pages.

Your eye will learn to see as little a space as half a point, equaling roughly $\frac{1}{144}$ of an inch. You will see at a glance where twenty-four point display type can be used rather than thirty point or perhaps eighteen point. All space on a layout page will seem as natural to your eyes and to your hand holding the pencil as the varying shades of gray produced by type. Some day, or perhaps even some night in your dreams, such terms as points, picas, trim size, etc., will be completely absorbed into your storehouse of technical information. You may pick up historical facts on type design ("italics" coming from the early Italian printers, for instance) and many other interesting facts on letter forms and on printing. You will know when you will want the crisp, direct impression of letterpress, and when to use the delicate method of offset printing with its astonishing accuracy. You will know how fast a carload of coated stock may be produced by your favorite paper mill, what sizes certain display faces come in, which typehouse has them, and you will even know what it will cost to do the stamping job as you visualize it. In brief, you will learn about the quality, the standard sizes and weights of book paper fitting standard presses as they are available to the American publisher. You will not only know display faces which are more or less easy to tell apart, such as san serif and script faces, but you will be able to recognize machine faces by certain characteristics, such as the lower loops of the lower case "g." You will know at a glance how wide a page is and what leading there is between the lines. You will guess quite accurately trim sizes and margins. Certainly you will have an opinion, one based on experience, on the quality of composition and presswork. In composition this may mean good word spacing, avoiding too many breaks at the end of the line and total avoidance of "rivers" (series of word spaces which form a visible line vertically or diagonally across a page). Good presswork is clean and even. Bad presswork is not. The many varieties of book cloth will not surprise you, especially since the manufacturers produce comparative grades.

As you look at the books you have designed, comparing them with others, you will see how your work matches up. Your own mistakes will become apparent to you, to others probably, too. But after a while, you will quite unconsciously have established a style of your own.

Different publishers usually have different needs according to the "list" they publish. At any rate, they have developed different methods, so the designer who has done a good job for a small publisher must change his approach in some ways when working for a larger house.

As you gain experience in book design, your mind will be constantly stimulated by your daily contact with books.

Just as you will continuously develop your own methods, you will simultaneously learn about machines, materials, and production methods. In fact, you will find that the more you learn about the means and techniques of production, the more you will want to learn. Plant visits will not just mean a good time but you will find that you are being taught much that you can benefit from in your own work.

Not everybody knows that books are printed on large presses. Even you, at the beginning of your career, will not be acquainted with definitive technical information, but eventually you will know how many thousand sheets some presses can turn out per hour. You will become interested in all machinery, and there is much of it used in the manufacture of books. You will visit paper mills and book-cloth manufacturers. You will observe the entire manufacture of typesetting equipment producing "hot" or "cold" composition. Perhaps you will be fascinated by the screeching sound of the routing machines spitting spirals of brass in the cutting of binders' dies.

Now you will know the intricacies of photoengraving, of camera work for offset printing; you will watch men correcting color plates, proofing them, and comparing the proofs to the original copy.

Of course, you will meet many artists, fine illustrators, and specialists in technical illustrations, diagrams, and the like. Their methods and techniques will be added to your growing understanding of how books should be illustrated.

The cost problem of illustrations—such as the artists' fees and the charges for engravings or plates —as well as that of presswork will become as familiar to you as the cost of routine composition. Even if you are not mechanically inclined, you will begin to understand the construction and the operation of the many machines which set, print and bind books. In effect, these machines represent multiple human brains and hands. Slow and tedious work such as setting type in a composing stick is translated into the rapid handling of the keys on the Linotype or Monotype machines. Their keyboards resemble, in principle, those of conventional typewriters. (With modern computers, type can be set at many times the speed human brains or hands could manage.)

Perhaps you know the principle of the oldest printing presses which made an impression from handset type possible on two or four pages. Today's power presses, running at tremendous speed, will print 128 pages simultaneously. The inking of the type is automatic, the supply of paper equally so. Their speed is a thousand times that of the beautiful miracle on which Gutenberg's forty-two line bible was printed over five hundred years ago. The time you spend in a pressroom trying to understand the construction and the workings of contemporary presses from a small 17" x 22" platen press to the enormous four-color "web" press will not be wasted. You will find that plant owners of printing and binding equipment will be happy to teach you as much of letterpress, offset, and gravure methods as you are willing and able to comprehend.

Folding machines pick up a printed sheet of 128 pages, fold it swiftly and accurately, and deliver four "signatures" of thirty-two pages each. Entire books printed and folded and separated in subsequent signatures are "collated" by a machine which sports as many as thirty to forty metal "hands." Every signature is sewn together with the preceding and succeeding signatures, and a seemingly unending stream of books is easily separated and bound and processed into its ultimate form by a succession of machines, each one designed to do, in fractions of seconds, what took bookbinders hours. Each of these machines is fascinating and worthwhile to watch.

Every part of this operation is fascinating. Equipment is constantly being improved and so you will watch the progress as it is being made. You will learn more and more. Kaleidoscopically, the methods and the machinery change and improve to produce this thing called Book.

But skills and machines are not all that create books. Ultimately, it is man who provides all creative and productive spirit to guide the written word from its very inception to its ultimate form as a book. So it is that many people are involved with the production of books, perhaps, in a manner of speaking, like the ground crew without whom the pilot cannot fly the passenger to his destination.

The author is not the only person who comes in contact with his manuscript. The manuscript is typed and retyped. It is edited and reedited. When it sounds all right to author and editor it has to be copy-edited.

In the meantime, many other people in the publishing house begin to take an interest in the manuscript which is about to be launched. The production manager begins to familiarize himself with the length and particular needs of the manuscript. The sales, as well as the publicity departments, happily dream of way to publicize and sell—hopefully—large quantities of a book yet unknown to the general public.

Perhaps now is the moment when the manuscript is handed to the designer. From here on it is his baby. It is now that the human element makes itself known to the designer. He may have conferences with the production department and with the editors, perhaps even with the author and the illustrator, if there is one. There will be telephone calls, perhaps even personal visits to the plant. People in the service department and even foremen in the plant will be drawn into the project.

The designer should, and usually does, plead for the best possible quality, perhaps also for schedules and promises. This will go on for no less than three months. Of course, in the meantime, work on other books has begun or is being intensified.

All this involves people. A good designer meets many people on both sides of the fence. If you are familiar with a person's interests and attitudes you may find it easier to discuss design or production problems with him. Thus, the occasional "crisis" can be resolved more easily, too.

If the designer—young and inexperienced in this business—should be inclined to make unreasonable demands or to be arrogant, he will learn very quickly that this is a fatal approach. There are one thousand and one ways in which even good designs can be spoiled or the life of a book designer can be filled with frustrations. Just as a book design becomes successful only when it is liked by the people for whom or with whom the designer works, so does his success in this field depend greatly on his personality.

Everyone who comes in contact with a designer and with his work must be treated with respect and friendliness, but also with understanding. The pace in book design and book production is very uneven. It may slow down a great deal but it can also accelerate tremendously. At such a time the people involved become harassed, nervous, and tense, so they must be handled with extra care.

Some of the people the designer deals with may have a drink with him or go out to lunch with him. At such times, a friendly personal contact, seemingly unmindful of the business at hand, can do wonders. You get your proofs faster, your corrections better, and perhaps even promises in regard to schedules and deliveries.

It is true that much of the aforementioned is the responsibility of the production department, but sometimes the designer acts for the production department or even as a production department.

The designer who becomes well acquainted with the many people working in the book industry at their varied jobs—who learns what they demand and what their talents are—can become and remain a friend to most of them. And in the process he may assure himself of a busy future in the trade.

As the many processes of learning in your chosen field go on and on, you will recognize that art, nature, and life itself have a direct relationship to what you produce. Anything you are learning, anything you interest yourself in, will eventually be useful to you. Your design will be the quintessence of all you know.